BASKETBALL:
Player Movement Skills

John M. Cooper, Ed.D.
Professor Emeritus
Indiana University
Bloomington, Indiana

Benchmark Press, Inc.
Indianapolis, Indiana

Library of Congress Cataloging in Publication Data:

COOPER, JOHN M., 1912--

BASKETBALL: PLAYER MOVEMENT SKILLS

Cover Design and Art: Craig Gosling

Cover Photo: Tom Rohyans

Library of Congress Catalog Card number: 86-71580

ISBN: 0-936157-11-9

Printed in the United States of America
10 9 8 7 6 5 4 3 2 1

Contents

CHAPTER 4 ANALYSES OF FUNDAMENTAL BASKETBALL SKILLS

CHAPTER 5 GAME TIME: PLAYER MOVEMENT SKILLS IN ACTION

FOREWORD

John Cooper was involved with the game of basketball the first time as a young boy when he constructed his own indoor and outdoor courts in the little town of Corydon, Kentucky. John played on a fine high school basketball team and continued an outstanding playing career at the University of Missouri. He was one of the first people to use the jump shot as an offensive scoring weapon. He has written several books and scientific articles on basketball while a professor at Indiana University's School of Health, Physical Education, and Recreation, and the director of its Biomechanics Laboratory.

John's greatest interest over the years has been the science of basketball presented in a practical manner. Many students have received great benefit from his research and work on many different things involved with basketball. He has helped many people develop sound philosophies regarding the teaching and coaching of the game. His thoughts on basketball are the result of extremely thorough research on his part. The depth of his investigations on the performance of players makes reading *BASKETBALL: PLAYER MOVEMENT SKILLS* a worthwhile undertaking.

I would enthusiastically recommend this book to anyone interested in the game of basketball. It has an extremely interesting approach to what makes the sport such a great game and has been put together by a man who has had a lifetime love affair with that game.

Bob Knight
Head Coach
Indiana University Basketball Team

ACKNOWLEDGEMENTS

I extend appreciation to Sharol Laczkowski for her original drawings made from film data and her review of some of the publications done in preparation for the writing of this book. Gratitude is also given to Charlianna Cooper for typing the manuscript and refining some of the original drawings. It would be an oversight not to mention Betty Haven, Kay Flatten, Ellen Burton, and Wynn Updyke, who read parts or all of the manuscript for technical or grammatical errors. Special recognition is given to college coaches Dean Sempert, of Lewis and Clark College, and Chuck Williams, of the University of Southern Missouri, for their contributions to the information concerning certain specific areas. Films made by James Richards at the University of Delaware in 1983 were used in the preparation of this book. Murray Bartow and Suzanne Miller posed for photographs from which several of the drawings in this book were made. Many of the figures in Chapter 4 were originally drawn from films made by Sharol Laczkowski. She also photographed several other shots for the book. Grateful thanks are offered to Wendy Bedingfield for her very careful reading of some of the manuscript, including suggestions for additions.

Finally, to all those coaches, athletes, and researchers who through the years have added to my knowledge, I acknowledge their contributions and influence.

January, 1987   John M. Cooper
                                                        Bloomington, Indiana

DEDICATION

To my brothers and sisters, namely Grant, Clay, Carma, Buty, and Mae; to my wife, Charlianna; and to all my former teammates and classmates at Corydon, Kentucky, High School.

This book is for players, coaches, fans, and students of the great game of basketball. I hope it will help players understand their skills and enable observers to comprehend various actions on the court. A word of caution, however.

Too much self-analysis by players may bring about paralysis. Mrs. Edward Craster, who published the following poem in the *Journal of Cassell's Weekly,* (part of Pinafore Press) in 1871 said it best.

> The centipede was happy quite
> until a toad in fun
> Said, "Pray, which leg goes
> after which?"
> That worked her mind to
> such a pitch,
> She lay distracted
> in a ditch
> Considering how to run.

PREFACE

Several of my peers and students have long urged me to put together a book on the physical principles involved in the skills of individual basketball players. My colleagues contended that after 20 years of playing and coaching the game at almost all levels, and more than 40 years of studying it, both practically and scientifically, I might have something worthwhile to contribute.

In 1969, I wrote *The Theory and Science of Basketball* with Daryl Siedentop. It contained some mechanical concepts, but was primarily concerned with the psychological and practical problems of teaching the game, devising plays, coaching, and administering. As a researcher in the field of kinesiology, I have published widely on biomechanics and related topics. Still, no one publication has drawn together all my thoughts about basketball from a performance perspective.

In undertaking this task, I had an opportunity to discover something new about the game of basketball. Writing has not only forced me to articulate my numerous theories and beliefs on the topic, but has presented a welcome occasion to do some original research in an effort to corroborate or refute some of the latest theories expounded by others.

The material in this book is intended for coaches, teachers, biomechanics experts, and top athletes, as well as once-a-week players and interested spectators. It is designed to be practical and understandable, even though technical matters are discussed.

In terms of organization, I introduced the material by presenting certain terms, selected principles, concepts for improvement, and procedures for movement analysis. There is also a chapter on the history of the game with some emphasis on the original mechanics of performance. It includes mention of some relatively unknown but great performers of the past.

This is followed by the discussion and application of certain physical principles that govern the actions of basketball players and an analysis of the fundamental moves made in the performance of basketball skills. Some of the information is quantitative in nature. Certain measurements are taken from film data. Finally, the actions of players in real game situations summarize the principles presented along with some new ones.

CHAPTER 1
Overview

As one devoted to scientific study, I use facts, phenomena, laws, and principles to investigate hypotheses and general laws subject to verification. A game such as basketball can be scientifically studied according to general principles of scientific inquiry.

Coaches and players frequently rely on empirical judgment to make decisions about many aspects of basketball. Their ideas are based on experience or observation. If nothing else is available, information based on the opinions of experienced individuals can be accepted until scientific investigations substantiate or refute the data.

In this book, I formulated principles whenever quantitative data were available. A number of principles presented in Cooper and Siedentop (3) were also used. The information in this chapter is an accumulation of concepts and ideas spanning many years. It focuses on moves of individual basketball players.

A discussion of individual basketball player movements, in order to be meaningful, involves more than physical principles. There is an interdependence among many influences and conditions that affects the outcome of actions. However, biomechanics, broadened to include physical principles and presented in understandable language, will be the major focus of this book. Motor learning procedures, applied psychological and anthropometric factors, and physical conditioning procedures may be mentioned briefly at times.

Strategy of play will be discussed only as it might affect the movements of a player or to present teaching and coaching theories. My intent is to stimulate interest in ideas that affect the movement of basketball players.

While the depth of discussion on certain areas may be somewhat restricted, players (from the rank beginner to the veteran), coaches (both novice and experienced), interested spectators, and biomechanics experts should discover enlightening insights.

The remainder of this chapter is devoted to orienting readers to a wide range of concepts regarding the movement of basketball players in action-packed environments.

RELATIONSHIP OF SCIENCE AND BIOMECHANICS TO BASKETBALL

The word biomechanics is a combination of bio-, meaning life, and mechanics, meaning forces causing motion. Thus, this is a study of forces produced by and acting on living bodies and an examination of how the forces affect motion.

The area of biomechanics involves the application of mechanical principles and factors related to locomotion in all living structures. Here, we examine the external and internal forces that act on basketball players and reveal the resulting effects.

Force is that which causes motion or acceleration or has the capacity to do so. It may stop motion as well. Two other words that have significance to biomechanics are: kinematics and kinetics. Kinematics is that portion of mechanics related to temporal and spatial characteristics without regard to forces such as acceleration, displacement, and velocity. (Acceleration is a time rate-of-change of velocity. A basketball player may run slowly, then quickly, or vice versa, to confuse an opponent. An added burst of speed may free an offensive player to take a shot at the basket. Displacement deals with player movement from one position to another on the floor. The path of the movement vectorially is the displacement. Velocity is a vector quantity denoting speed in a given direction. Vectors are quantities that have magnitude and direction.) Kinetics is that branch of mechanics related to the forces producing or modifying motion, such as when the foot contacts the floor in jumping.

Finally, the terms qualitative and quantitative should be explained in this context. In a biomechanical sense, qualitative means a relative assessment, such as one player is taller than another. Quantitative relates to exact measures, such as how much taller one player is than another. The former is a relative concept; the latter is a precise measurement.

LEARNING AND PERFORMANCE

Understanding athletic movements is a complex process for several reasons.

1) Usually athletes do not know or cannot describe what they do in performing skills. They often perform intuitively. It is an asset for a player to perform a skill without thinking about it. (See Chapter 4 for further treatment of this statement.)

2) Men and women perform skills in about the same way. While there are slight differences in height, strength, and speed, feats performed only by men years ago are now accomplished by women. For example, women basketball players can now dunk the ball and hang in the air.

3) Good form today is often unacceptable tomorrow. A debt is owed to performers of the past upon whom present performances are based. At one point, the two-hand set shot in basketball was considered the ultimate in mechanical execution.

4) Coaches make statements about performance that are usually correct, but at times may be incorrect. Athletes may execute plays in accordance with coaches' dictates, which could be wrong. Some actions advocated by coaches may be impossible to perform; consequently, the athletes may have to perform otherwise without being aware of it. Coaching instructions are frequently based on experience, and not necessarily on scientifically or experimentally proven information. However, as new facts become known, the intelligent coach makes use of them.

5) Any person, regardless of height, speed, or strength, should be regarded as a potential basketball player. Even with such deficiencies as small hands, slowness, short legs, and poor jumping ability, individuals can become good players.

Prenatal influences help mold the final human movement patterns, but they are not absolute determinants. Undirected basketball play in childhood may also affect behavior on the court in later years. New ways of moving and shooting in basketball are often developed in undisciplined and unsupervised environments. The so-called "playground" moves may be incorporated later in the play of disciplined, team-oriented players.

Being able to focus during performance on an aspect of a movement is called "the high point of attention." Usually, a performer is only able to think of one change at a time, certainly no more than two. It would be much better to have all the moves automatic.

The brain orders a certain movement to take place, but it leaves the execution of the action to lower levels of the nervous system. In other words, to be automatic in a basketball skill, conscious thought is not utilized. It is very difficult to change the form of a player after reaching the college level. As the saying goes, "Bad habits die hard."

PERFORMANCE CONCEPTS

• Player movements executed the same way every time can become so familiar to others that they may become easy to defend against.

• After a performer starts a movement, it is difficult to stop. Yet, a controlled movement intended to deceive can be stopped because it is often done with submaximal effort.

• The offensive player knows what is intended in a given moment and should have the advantage over the defensive player.

• In basketball, the desired strength and speed may not be attained in practice and during games. Additional exercises and speed maneuvers may be necessary.

• Flexibility is important for basketball players. They should focus on flexibility exercises for the pelvis, back, legs, and arms.

• Players are one-eyed and one-footed. The dominant eye's role in shooting is evident as the head turns slightly to one side or the other (7). Also, one particular foot is often used in the first step in driving by the defensive player.

THE COACH AS OBSERVER AND CORRECTOR

Basketball coaches, who spend considerable time observing players' actions, should follow these guidelines.

1) The human eye sees action at about 10 to 12 frames per second (fps). Very fast action is difficult to observe. First determine the action of the large body parts. Then the movements of small parts, such as the hand, can be partially seen.

2) Several viewings of a motion are necessary, because you can see only one body part at a time.

3) Coaches may get too close to a player, blurring the view. Move back and look "through" players and occasionally look out of the corners of your eyes. While peripheral vision picks up action sooner than direct vision, it does not usually perceive color or a clear image of action.

4) Fight the tendency to see what you expect.

4

5) Observe from many vantage points: from above, from the rear, at a distance, and close up.

The outstanding coaches understand and can teach mechanics, or they hire staff members who serve in this capacity. The proper time, however to teach correct mechanical moves in fundamental skills is when players are young, yet strong enough to execute properly. Coaches must also encourage innovative and creative play early on.

Players must master good mechanics. However, since many of them practice until a skill becomes automatic, the coach often becomes the corrector. There are a few players who realize when mechanical errors are made. As they view film, they see mistakes. The younger the player, the easier it is to correct flaws. It may take at least one or two years to eradicate serious errors in older players, when improvement is possible.

Because of the tendency to play instinctively, many great players have difficulty coaching. They often cannot describe what they do or what they want their players to do. They also tend to be impatient. Top coaches must be able to spend much time restudying the game and must have experienced both success and defeat. This makes the player who becomes a coach humble enough to encourage a slow learner. A good coach must sacrifice his or her ego, which may be difficult for a former star.

THE STUDY OF BASKETBALL ACTIONS

Basketball involves several skills, including running, jumping, and throwing. These are similar to but not identical to actions found in track and field and other sports. The dimensions of the court (approximately 90 by 50 feet and smaller in half court play) and the presence of 10 players necessitate modification of movements used in all out efforts. Emphasis is on quickness, coupled with deception, in anticipation of subsequent actions. Some experts believe top basketball players are the best all around athletes in the world.

A player may make a move that is mechanically unsound to deceive an opponent or execute without interference. For example, an offensive player may take off in a layup on the wrong foot to prevent an opponent from blocking the shot. Mechanics can be sacrificed for deception.

The importance of proper mechanical execution, however, cannot be overstated. Players who are consistent in correctly performing particular moves are usually successful. This does not mean that a good player is a mechanical player. Rather, it means that a successful player performs consistently according to certain physical laws and principles.

Psychological, physiological, sociological, and moral factors influence player performance. Some coaches believe that psychological factors are four times more influential than physical factors in determining the outcome of a game. I believe that if desire and determination are equal among similarly skilled players, then the more mechanically correct individuals are usually victorious.

The word "momentum" is often used as depicting the possible winner. While it is true that the player with the greatest confidence has the advantage of the moment, this can be offset by an opponent's adherence to sound execution of the fundamentals, particularly on defense.

RHYTHM AND MOVEMENT

Rhythm and tempo are important in player performance. If the normal tempo of a team is disrupted, the players often play poorly. If a slow-breaking team is forced by the use of a press to move faster than normal, play may be adversely affected. A normally fast-moving team can become impatient if the opposing team holds the ball as long as possible before shooting.

The rhythm of a player in a layup is recorded in Figure 1-1 (2, p. 166). Interference by the opposition could cause the rhythm to change.

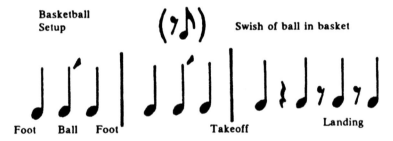

Figure 1-1. The rhythm of a basketball player shooting a layup, recorded in musical notes.

To disturb the rhythm of a player or team, an opponent tries to force hurried shots, moves that are too fast, and mechanically unsound actions. The victim may panic and jump, pass, or run in unusual ways. The muscles may tighten under stress, preventing the execution of correct mechanics. Confidence can be lost. Opponents who use the full court press and effective trapping procedures frequently create rhythm disturbances.

CHAPTER **2**

Early History of The Game

An account of the early history of the game of basketball may seem out of place in a book concerned with biomechanics and physical principles. Yet, many moves, including the jump shot and tip–in, have evolved either by accident or necessity due to certain rules or playing conditions. For example, the 3–second rule in the key area (instituted in 1932) forced players to execute more rapidly than they had previously. The hook, jump, and fadeaway shots became successful ways in which to release the ball in a hurry.

Some basketball history buffs believe the manner in which the game is played in a given period reflects society at the time. For example, in an agrarian society, players and spectators expected slow, methodical play, but in the jet age, fast play and spectacular moves are the norm.

Occasionally a player from one generation makes a move that may come to fruition in another age. Coaches may also use techniques from the past that current players are unprepared to combat.

Most new moves in basketball were invented by players in uninhibited playing conditions. They have been allowed to try new moves and have made them often enough to become automatic. Coaches seldom invent new ways to perform basketball skills. The great coaches recognize the merits of a new technique and encourage its refinement.

The contemporary setting, with national television exposure, has eliminated many secrets. Ingenious use of computers opens the possibility that plays can be developed in theory without players. Using film of a player, computers can manipulate the player's velocity, arm and leg movements, and height of jumps. New theories can be tested in practice.

Since history is a systematic record of past events, historical writers have to make decisions about including certain occurrences and excluding others. In this chapter I have followed that process and recorded certain facts (some for the first time) that have bearing on the mechanics of actions used by early players.

There are interesting differences between play in small towns and in cities. The eastern United States, where the game had its birth, developed a style that was emulated for some time. Gradually, men's play west of the Ohio and Mississippi rivers became faster, more open, and less conventional. These players developed the fast break and the jump shot.

This chapter will describe the styles of players who were not widely known in the eastern United States. They made great contributions to the game.

Players of one era cannot be compared easily to those of another. There are too many variables, including facilities, training procedures, and rule changes. It is clear, however, that current players owe much to their predecessors. Barriers have been broken and new ideas have been firmly entrenched.

Today's players have a firm base on which to build with their own creativity and innovation.

INVENTION OF THE GAME

Archaeologists have found that balls or objects with goals were used as games by the Mayans, Incas, and Aztec Indians. The same is true of the ancient Egyptians. The goal was vertical, rather than horizontal. The size of the field was probably several acres; the number of players probably unlimited.

Dr. James Naismith, a native Canadian of Scottish ancestry, invented the game of basketball in 1891 at the Young Men's Christian Association's (YMCA) International Training School in Springfield, Massachusetts. Known as one of the very few truly American sports, basketball was created to fulfill a need for enjoyable exercise and recreation.

As a youngster, Naismith was an orphan who worked hard on his uncle's small Canadian farm. He played many games with neighborhood boys, but one game that would influence his ideas about basketball was "Duck on the Rock." In it, one player would guard his duck from stones thrown by others.

Naismith was graduated from McGill University in Canada as a theologian. While at McGill he participated in gymnastics and football (English rugby). Upon graduation, he came to the United States where he began training to become a physical director. He played American football at the training school in Springfield under A.A. Stagg, one of the great football coaches. After one year of study, Naismith was appointed to the faculty.

During 1891 it became evident to the school's director, Dr. Luther Gulick, and the faculty that some form of organized winter recreation was needed. The Swedish, French, and German systems of physical education were tried, but were not "interesting, easy to learn, and easy to play in the winter and by artificial light." (2, p. 83) Naismith's colleagues tried to modify gymnastic games, medicine ball games, cricket, and apparatus activities, but all failed to gain the interest of the students, who were mature men. (At that time, the school trained two classes of leaders: physical directors and secretaries.)

Naismith started by modifying rugby and American football, but both were failures for indoor play. Soccer was not suited to a small space, and lacrosse adaptations were too brutal for indoor use. Finally, he decided on a new game with the following criteria. (2, p.62)

1. There must be a ball. It should be large, light, and handled with the hands.

2. There shall be no running with the ball.

3. No man on either team shall be restricted from getting the ball at any time it is in play.

4. Both teams are to occupy the same area, yet there is to be no personal contact.

5. The goal shall be horizontal and elevated.

Key elements of the five basic rules derived from American football, and the use of a large ball had its origin in soccer. The rough play inherent in these games, however, was to be eliminated. As in soccer, the "keep away" aspects were dominant. The "Duck on the Rock" game had taught Naismith that "when the rock was thrown in an arc, accuracy was more effective than force." Consequently, he thought of an elevated goal. (2, p.50)

English rugby influenced the start of play, but instead of throwing the ball between two lines of forward players, Naismith decided to throw the ball up between one player from each team. This was the beginning of the center jump.

It happened that the superintendent of buildings at the school was asked for two boxes to be used as goals. Having none, he suggested two old peach baskets instead. These were attached to the "lower rail of the balcony, one at either end of the gym." (2, p.53) The basket was placed 10 feet above the floor, the present height of the goal. Since there was no hole in the bottom of the basket, it was necessary for someone to climb up a ladder to retrieve the ball if it entered the basket. "After a successful goal the ball would have to be pushed, lifted or by the use of a cord, jerked out of the basket." (4, p.8)

There were 18 men in Naismith's class, nine on each team. In the small gymnasium, frequent collisions could cause injuries, so every effort was made to eliminate roughness. The original rules appear in Table 2-1.

Table 2-1. Original Basketball Rules

Below are Naismith's original 13 rules for basketball. It is obvious they helped establish the physical principles that are still evident today.

1. The ball may be thrown in any direction with one or both hands.
2. The ball may be batted in any direction with one or both hands (never with the fist).
3. A player cannot run with the ball. The player must throw it from the spot on which he catches it; allowance to be made for a man who catches the ball when running at a good speed.
4. The ball must be held in or between the hands; the arms or body must not be used for holding it.
5. No shouldering, holding, pushing, tripping, or striking, in any way the person of an opponent shall be allowed; the first infringement of this rule by any person shall count as a foul, the second shall disqualify him until the next goal is made, or, if there was evident intent to injure the person for the whole game, no substitute allowed.
6. A foul is striking at the ball with the fist, violation of Rules 3, 4, and such as described in Rule 5.
7. If either side makes three consecutive fouls, it shall count as a goal for the opponents. (Consecutive means without the opponents in the meantime making a foul.)

Table 2-1. (continued)

8. A goal shall be made when the ball is thrown or batted from the grounds into the basket and stays there, providing those defending the goal do not touch or disturb the goal. If the ball rests on the edge and the opponent moves the basket, it shall count as a goal.

9. When the ball goes out of bounds, it shall be thrown into the field and played by the person touching it. In case of a dispute, the umpire shall throw it straight into the field. The thrower-in is allowed five seconds. If he holds it longer, it shall go to the opponent. If any side persists in delaying the game, the umpire shall call a foul on them.

10. The umpire shall be judge of the men and shall note the fouls and notify the referee when three consecutive fouls have been made. He shall have power to disqualify men according to Rule 5.

11. The referee shall be the judge of the ball and shall decide when the ball is in play, in bounds, to which side it belongs, and shall keep the time. He shall decide when a goal has been made, and keep account of the goals, with any other duties that are usually performed by a referee. 12. There shall be two fifteen minute halves, with five minutes rest in between.

13. The side making the most goals in that time shall be declared the winners. In case of a draw, the game may, by agreement of the captains, be continued until another goal is made. (2, p.52)

The first game played in the class included three forwards, three centers, and three backs on each team. (2, p.95) Upon making a foul, a player was confined to the sideline until the next goal was scored. In the early years, no number of fouls would eliminate a player.

Naismith mentioned that a player would pause with the ball held overhead, concentrating on making a goal. Figures 2-1 to 2-3 show shooting positions probably common in the early game and show how certain techniques derived from other sports skills.

Figure 2-1. A toss at the basket, similar to the soccer throw from out-of-bounds. These are conceptual representations since there are no pictures or statements about early shooting styles.

Figure 2-2. A toss at the basket, similar to a shot put throw.

Figure 2-3. Shooting style similar to a rugby pass, from which the underhand shot developed.

Basketball owes much to the YMCA, not only because the game began at its training school, but also because the Y preserved basketball's identity, promoted it throughout the nation and world, and fostered its early growth. The American Athletic Union (AAU) and athletic clubs arranged games; by 1897, there were 58 clubs with organized teams.

Naismith believed that high schools accepted basketball before colleges. He thought high school boys played the game at the YMCA and took their skills on to schools and colleges.

One of the first states to adopt a high school basketball program was Indiana. Today, "Hoosier Hysteria" for basketball is a nationally recognized passion, and former Indiana players are active with collegiate and professional teams across the country. A legendary small-town team's victory in a 1954 state championship is the basis for the 1986 motion picture titled "Hoosiers."

EARLY RULE CHANGES

While the rules in some instances have been changed, the basic concepts remain in effect. This section will discuss only important early rules and how rule changes affected the game and the performance of players.

According to Menke, from 1902 until 1915, there were as many as five main sets of rules as well as local modifications, including a lack of uniformity in interpretations of the rules (1, p. 161). During this period, most officials did not disqualify a player unless unnecessary roughness was noted continuously. It is easy to understand how spectators viewed basketball as similar to rugby and soccer, in which rough play was common.

The AAU joined with the YMCA early to participate in a rule-making and governing body. The National Federation of State High School Athletic Associations and the Canadian Amateur Basketball Association joined the rules and governing body between 1929 and 1939.

The period from 1932–33 to 1936–37 produced some far-reaching changes in the rules. One was the 10-second rule, designed to cut down on stalling by dividing the court into equal halves with a center line. The offensive team was required to cross the center line in 10 seconds after gaining possession. This quickened the pace of the game and encouraged clever dribblers and great shooters.

(I participated in a Missouri-Kansas game where the Kansas defense was set up in a deep zone. Our coach wanted us to hold the ball if we got an early lead and force the Kansas players to guard further out on the court. Kansas Coach Forrest "Phog" Allen called it a "stratified-transitional" zone defense. Our guards brought the ball across the center of the court almost every time we had possession, but Kansas refused to come out of its zone until the last minute of the first half and near the end of the game. Missouri won, 26-22.)

There were a few other instances in other parts of the country where offensive teams held the ball for a considerable time without attempting to score. Naismith stated that the Kansas City AAU Stage Lines in 1934 stalled with the ball 12 minutes and passed 343 times without attempting to make a goal.

The stalling problem became so acute by 1939–40 that the offended team was awarded a free throw (originating from the penalty shot in soccer and other games). It could be waived and the ball could be taken out of bounds instead to be put into play at mid-court.

The second major change was limiting the time offensive players could station themselves with the ball in the free throw lane. Later, any offensive player was prohibited from being in this area more than three seconds. Some old time coaches have told me privately that this change was made by a few coaches on the committee to handicap a good offensive player who had some years left to play on an opposing team. Rule changes were sometimes proposed by individuals for personal rather than professional motives; however, many changes turned out to benefit the game.

Early on, there were nine men on a team (Figure 2-4). This continued for about three years, then five men were allowed on the court in small gymnasiums and nine only in large gyms. The rule allowing five men per team on the floor was established in 1897. At first, substitutions were not allowed unless a player left the game and did not re-enter. By 1953-54, unlimited substitutions were permitted.

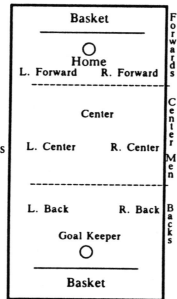

Figure 2-4.
Positions of the Players
(Naismith, *Basketball*,
p. 95)

In the 1902-03 rules, a ball could go out-of-bounds and not be considered out of play if it bounced back into the court area. Also, if the ball was out of bounds and the official was unable to tell who touched the ball last, the first player to touch it was allowed to throw it in bounds.

In some of the gyms at that time, there would be a running track around the balcony. When a ball was knocked up on the running track, there would be a mad scramble for the stairways leading up to the balcony. Frequently, fights would break out when as many as 10 players attempted to reach the ball in the balcony. (4, p.8 and 9; also in 2, p.67 and 69)

There were zone markings on the court in the early 1920s in the men's game. Teams included a running guard, a standing guard, a standing forward, a running forward, and a center used primarily as a jumper rather than a scorer. A few years later the center became an integral part of the offense and defense.

Most of the rule changes from this time on, with the exception of the 3-second and 10-second rules, were for clarification and interpretation. In general, rule changes reflected the fact that as defensive players caught up with offensive players, new offensive moves were developed. Eventually, rules for these adaptations had to be developed. There were slight modifications of court markings, provisions for time outs, inclusion of high schools in the governing bodies, equipment changes, and changes in the number of officials and time outs permitted.

I played during several seasons in college and in the AAU where only one official was used. This enabled a player to hold or push an opponent without being seen by the official. During this era, a slow defensive player could grab the bottom of a fast offensive player's trunks to slow him down. A defensive player could grasp an offensive player tightly enough to prevent a tip-in or rebound. Arms could be clamped to prevent a player from catching the ball.

The Dribble

Very early in basketball history, the dribble was considered a defensive move. When the player with the ball was closely guarded by opposing players, he bounced or rolled the ball on the floor and then retrieved it to escape. Four years after basketball's invention, the dribble became an integral part of the game.

Some early rules on dribbling were changed. One such rule in 1901 was that a player could not dribble and then shoot at the goal. This was changed in 1908 to allow a player to shoot for a basket after a dribble. For a while, a player could dribble overhead as he advanced down the court. Again, rule changes eliminated this maneuver by calling it an infraction.

Dribbling skills of the past and present are depicted in Figures 2-5 to 2-7.

Figure 2-5.
Dribbling technique (as well as guarding position of the 1920s)

Figure 2-6.
Modern between-the-legs dribble.

Figure 2-7.
Modern behind-the-back dribble.

Guarding

The early concept of guarding allowed the defensive player to hold his ground but avoid interfering with an offensive player's shot execution (Figure 2-8). The present day guarding allows defensive players to interfere with dribbling and shooting (Figure 2-9).

Figure 2-8.
Guarding position on the court in the 1920's.

Figure 2-9.
Present day guarding out on the court.

Free Throws

The rule on a free throw awarded after a foul has changed very little from the original. At one time, the best free thrower made all free throw attempts for his team. In the 1923-24 season the rule was changed to read:

When a personal foul is called, the player against whom the foul is committed must attempt the free throw or throws; that requirement holds unless the player entitled to the free throw is injured, in which event the substitute must attempt the throw. (4, p.47)

The players shot from the free throw line in an underhand technique (Figure 2-10). Some players and researchers still think it is the most accurate way to shoot a foul shot.

Figure 2-10. Underhand foul shot, 1920s-1940s.

Center Jump

During the early 1900s, the basketball was put into play to start each half and after a successful goal with a center jump. Figure 2-11 portrays court dimensions and player positions in 1915-16.

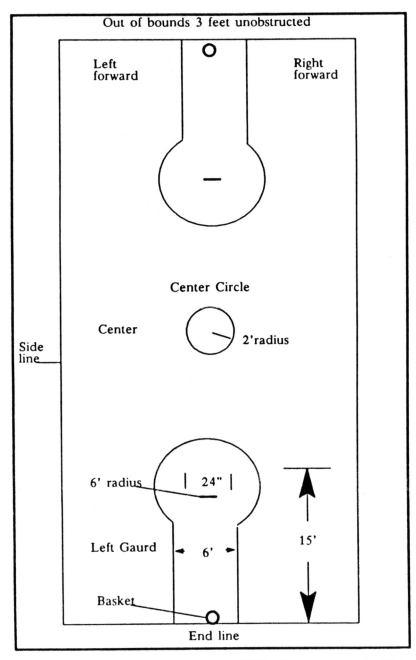

Figure 2–11. Basketball court for the 1915–16 season (4, P. 35)

This center jump practice continued until a 1935-36 rule change stating that the ball was to be put in play from the out-of-bounds endline by the team scored upon. This began the end of the center jump after a goal. The 1937-38 edition of Spalding's Official Basketball Guide stated, "After a goal from the field, any player of the team scored upon shall put the ball into play from any point out-of-bounds at the end of the court where the goal was made." (3, p. 61)

The elimination of the center jump put more emphasis on speedup play and led to the present day fast break, in which an offensive player attempts to drive to the basket before the defensive players are set.

The center jump is now used only at the beginning of the game and at each overtime period. This too may become a thing of the past. The original rules called for the ball to be tossed higher than the players could jump. The present centers are so much taller than the officials that it is almost impossible to throw the ball high enough for a fair jump. The ball is usually struck by one of the centers on its upward flight in a seldom-called infraction. Jump ball rules for women are now the same as men's.

The Pivot

The movement of a player after he has dribbled, stopped, and picked up the ball is called the pivot. It evolved from early rules, which allowed a player to turn with the ball if he kept one foot in place, rather than run or dribble. This lowering and turning of the body became a basic skill of the game, and although it is more refined now, it is an integral part of individual player movement.

Coach Meanwell at the University of Wisconsin became known in the 1920s for his style of pivot and pass (handoff) game. He had his players move, stop, turn, and give the ball to a teammate as the group moved almost the length of the court. It was a difficult offensive team maneuver to combat at that time.

Equipment

Naismith stated that the only pieces of equipment that are "accidental" in origin are the backboards (2, p.98). Spectators at early games were often seated in the gallery. Since the baskets were nailed to the balconies' lower edges, it was fairly easy for a fan to reach through and guide a ball into or away from a basket, or to shake a ball out of a basket. (Originally, the ball had to stay in the basket to be a scored goal.)

To combat this problem, six by four feet backboards made of screen or other solid material were required by the rules. These dimensions are still in effect today. Officials eventually decided that the screen was unsatisfactory because of its looseness and lack of resistance, so plate glass backboards were introduced in 1909. Wooden backboards, painted white, replaced the glass ones in 1916. Many courts, regardless of the rules, had no glass backboards, and a team that practiced with wooden backboards was at a disadvantage rebounding when it played on a court with glass ones. It was not until after World War II that glass was widely used again.

Court Facilities

Basketball buffs speculate that teams playing on courts where there were pillars within the court area introduced blocking, screening, and picking to basketball. My high school's team played on a court above a garage. It was common for the offensive team to try to "rub–off" defensive players on the roof supports as they moved about the court.

Some early courts had ceilings no higher than the backboards, especially in small communities. This made shooting at the basket difficult. The ball had to be released at a low angle of trajectory. (See Trajectory in Chapter 3.)

Many small town schools had only outdoor courts. Wind sometimes made it impossible to shoot long shots. Some early basketballs had outseams to withstand the grinding effects of the dirt courts.

Most teams, particularly independent ones, played in any available gymnasium. Spectator room was limited, so the entire playing court area might be enclosed as a cage. Under these conditions, there was no out-of-bounds. The ball was always in play. Some unusual maneuvers were instituted under these circumstances.

I watched such a game in the 1929–30 season between two black high schools. A net surrounded the court on two sides, and the players threw the ball against the front and rear walls and the ceiling, retrieving it on the rebound. They even climbed the wall at each end to throw the ball through the goal.

Some gymnasiums had both low ceilings and concrete floors. The floor could become very slick. It was always hard on the legs and caused abrasions. Players employed protective body mechanics by maintaining wide bases with their feet, arms, and legs set to ward off blows. They ran upright with short steps.

WOMEN AND THE GAME

Naismith said that although basketball originated in an all-male setting, women teachers at a nearby grade school wanted to play (2, p.161). He invited them to try.

Before long, a women's team was formed at the training center to play against another team (Figure 2-12). The game spread rapidly to other eastern colleges and to the west coast. It had moved into the high schools by the late 1800s.

Figure 2-12.
Young lady shooting a one hand shot. Perhaps women were the first to actually use a one hand shot. It is reported that this style of shooting was adopted because the women wore corsets and could not turn their bodies very much. Other styles of shooting were thought to be too masculine. This is drawn from a picture of material in the archives of Tulane University. Clara Bare is the author of the *Sophie Newcomb Memorial College for Women, Basketball Rules for Women and Girls,* Printed in 1895 in New Orleans, Louisiana.

Rita Walker was one of the great women players in the midwest in the 1930s. She could pass, dribble, guard, and shoot as well as any male player. At about the same time there was a women's team known as the "Red Heads" that traveled around the midwest playing men's teams as equals.

Rules for the women's game, developed from the men's rules, were adopted in 1898.(2, p.166).

1. The ball could not be taken away from the player who was holding it.

2. The player in possession of the ball could not hold it for longer than three seconds.

3. The floor was divided into three sections (Figure 2-13), and a player could not cross these lines under penalty of a foul.

4. A defending player could not reach over another player who was in possession of the ball. The arms must be kept in a vertical-lateral plane, and a violation of this rule by a defensive player was called overguarding.

There were two calibers of women's play: one in which the women played the three-section court, and the other in which women played according to men's rules. In a few places in the country, women's teams played almost entirely by the men's rules.

There were often six team members on the floor with a jumping center and a running center and the guards and forwards staying in their territories. Scoring was done by forwards, usually the best shooters.

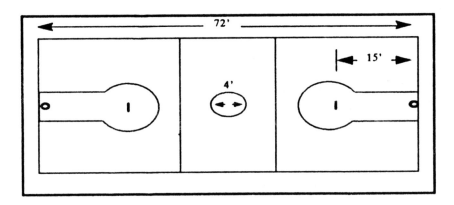

Figure 2-13. Diagram of Woman's 3-section basketball court. From Spalding's *Women's Basketball Guide*.

Males were rarely allowed to watch females practice. Usually the teams had separate courts. On game days, however, the girls played the preliminary game, which was viewed by spectators of both sexes.

While basketball grew in popularity, many schools had dropped the sport for women by 1930, due in part to a stand taken by Mrs. Theodore Roosevelt that certain games were too strenuous for girls and women.[1] This included basketball.

However, a few states, such as Iowa [2] kept competitive basketball at the high school level. Most colleges maintained the sport at the intramural level.

Decades later, basketball and other women's sports returned to schools and colleges. Without a long history of high-level basketball playing, however, the skills of the girls and women were not as refined as those of their male counterparts. Women are now rapidly closing the gap. They generally play according to men's rules, with slight modifications. In a few years they will be equal to the men in skill, but probably not in strength and speed.

In July 1985, three women, Senda Abbott, Bertha Teague, and Martha Wade were enshrined in the Basketball Hall of Fame in Springfield, Massachusetts. Abbott is called the "mother of women's basketball." She worked with Naismith on the first official rules for women and introduced the sport at Smith College in 1893. Teague was a great high school coach, and Wade an outstanding coach at the college level.

DEVELOPMENT OF NEW SKILLS

I have been credited as being among the very first players to use a jump shot as a primary scoring technique. Since I was smaller but quicker than most high school players in 1928, I began shooting after receiving a pass while up in the air. This allowed me to take a shot unmolested before returning to the floor.

A new way of shooting enjoys a period of freedom before the defense catches on. To receive the ball from a pass or to dribble and move to a location with the ball, then jump into the air, was a natural evolution and refinement. A two-hand jump shot gradually became a one-hand shot.

1. From Professor Mary Lou Remley, Indiana University.
2. Girls' rules in several states used restrictive three playing areas in which there were six players on each team instead of five who were not permitted outside their zones of operation. Forwards did all the scoring under these rules.

In the two-hand shots(Figure 2-14),the dominant hand left the ball last, so it was an easy transition to true one-hand shooting. It was a matter of time before the two-hand set shot became the one-hand set shot such as that used by Chuck Hyatt of the University of Pittsburgh and AAU teams in the late 1920s and the 1930s. He was the first to use the one-hand set shot as a regular shot from the field, although he starts the shot lower than do players of today.

Figure 2-14. Hand position for two-hand set shot, 1940s.

An investigation I conducted in 1937 revealed that several of the players in the then Big Six Conference (now the Big Eight) shot regularly from a distance of 25 to 30 feet. The results showed:

1. The players attempted 50 percent or less shots during a game than the modern players, but they shot from a longer distance.

2. More shots were taken from the right side of the floor than from the left.

3. Twenty-five feet from the basket was the most accurate distance, except for very close-in shots.

4. No shots were attempted from the deep corners of the court.

5. Many shots were attempted from the right side at a 30-degree angle, so the ball could be banked off the backboard.

The differences in the areas from where shots were attempted were:
1. The two-hand shot can be launched at a longer distance from the basket than can the jump shot, with reasonable accuracy.
2. The jump shot, now practically the only shot used, is more accurate within 15 feet than the two-hand set shot.

EARLY TEAMS AND PLAYERS

In such cities as New York, where the Celtics had their home base, mechanics were established for the 1920s and 1930s. These included shooting the two-hand set shot, executing the weaving dribble, perfecting ball handling, passing, and center play. Several players later took head coaching jobs at major colleges, including Joe Lapchick, who coached at St. Johns, and Nat Holman, who led the City College of New York (CCNY) team.

Some ex-high school and college players became professional and semi-professional players in Indiana, with the Fort Wayne Pistons pro team, and in Wisconsin, with the Sheyboygan Red Skins, who was the premier team at one time. Rochester and Syracuse, New York, also had professional teams in the 1940s.

Through the years, however, the AAU attracted the best players. Strong ex-college players made up teams for the Kansas City Athletic Club; the Cooke Paint and Varnish Company of Kansas City; The St. Joseph, Missouri, Hilyards; and the Wichita, Kansas, Henrys. Later, the Denver Piggley-Wiggleys, the Kansas City Stage Liners, and the Phillips 66ers of Bartlesville, Oklahoma, were among strong teams of the 1930s. Most cities had AAU or independent town teams.

George Mikan of DePaul University in Chicago was selected as the player of the period 1900-1950. He and Bob Kurland of Oklahoma A and M (now Oklahoma State) were among the first big men to play the game, both being just under seven feet tall. Mikan had a hook shot that smaller centers could not stop.

The player second to Mikan in the voting was Chuck Hyatt. He was much more versatile than Mikan, being a fine passer, dribbler, and shooter.

Experts believe that Forrest "Red" DeBarnadi, who played in the 1920s and 1930s, was one of the greatest players of all time. A student at tiny Westminster College in Fulton, Missouri, he is the only All-American in any sport selected from that school.

In 1927 I saw DeBarnadi play for the Cooke Paint and Varnish Company of Kansas City against an AAU team in Evansville, Indiana. He shot goals (two-hand and underhand) from near center court, dribbled with a weave through many players, and rebounded with authority at both ends of the court. He passed the ball with deception and played good defense. He was an early edition of today's Larry Bird.

Some people would argue that Jack McCracken of Missouri Maryville College (now Northwest State) was the greatest player of all time. Certainly he should receive recognition, since he was an All-American AAU player at forward, center, and guard. Hank Iba was his college coach.

Some basketball devotees credit Hank Luisette of Stanford with inventing the one-hand set shot and the jump shot. Since Chuck Hyatt used the one-hand set shot earlier, and others (including myself) used the jump shot before Luisette's time, it appears that his contribution consisted of refinement and popularization. Glenn Roberts, a player from Pound, Virginia, used the jump shot in 1930.

I cannot verify who first used the fadeaway jump shot. Clay Cooper, from the University of Missouri, used a fadeaway one-hand jump shot in the late 1930s. He may have been the first.

The Harlem Globe Trotters team, formed in 1928 and composed of great black players, displayed superb ball handling skills. "Goose" Tatum was as fine an offensive player as had appeared at the time. The Globe Trotters served as role models for young blacks who wanted to play. (The first black basketball player at Indiana University was Bill Garrett from 1949 to 1951. No other school in the Big Nine Conference – now the Big Ten – had a black player at that time.)

All members of the Stanford University team that came to the NCAA tournament in 1942 could shoot one-hand set shots. They won the championship and helped to establish this technique throughout the country. The east teams were the last to adopt the one-hand set and the jump shots. One New York City coach threatened to quit coaching if he had to teach the one-hand foul shots he saw western team members practicing. He had to change his thinking as the shot became universally accepted.

Professional basketball did not become a permanent and widespread part of the basketball scene in most parts of the United States until after World War II. Television now displays the skills of the best pro players (usually ex-college team members), sometimes to the chagrin of high school and college coaches, who are still molding younger players. Some professional play is for show, and certain styles are unique to individuals and cannot be widely imitated.

COACHES OF THE PAST

Out of each section of the country, great coaches have risen. This section will describe some who were active through the 1930s, 1940s, and just beyond. Most have been shrewd judges of raw talent and great recruiters. They have been, for the most part, inventors of formations and team maneuvers.

H.C. Carlson, M.D., coach at the University of Pittsburgh in the 1930s and 1940s, invented the "figure eight." This, along with the shuffle offense, was the forerunner of the motion offense now used so successfully by Bob Knight at Indiana University. (The shuffle offense was created at the University of Oklahoma by an assistant, Jerome "Shocky" Needy, who had been asked by the head coach – the late Bruce Drake – to come up with a new formation. Each player on offense moved to all the positions on the court during offensive maneuvers.)

Kansas University's "Phog" Allen, who coached from 1925 to 1950 and is considered by many to be history's most outstanding coach, was a master recruiter, superb motivator, early exponent of transition play, and great executor of high level skills. During halftimes he would sometimes challenge opposing coaches to shoot baskets. If he failed to entice his adversary, he would put on a personal exhibition. He was a showman in a class by himself.

Everett Dean, an Indiana University product who went from coaching at IU (1925–1938) to Stanford (1939–1955), led teams that were masters of precision and exponents of new maneuvers.

Adolph Rupp, who played for Allen at Kansas, had great coaching success at the University of Kentucky from 1930 to 1972. He was regarded as an excellent recruiter.

Teams coached by Claire Bee of Long Island University were great zone players and displayed classic east coast style. Between the 1940s and the 1960s, Bee perfected the best methods of defeating zone teams.

Hank Iba, who played at Westminister College in Missouri, was considered the best defensive coach of his era. He coached at several colleges, including Oklahoma A & M (now Oklahoma State University), and his disciplinary approach was so successful that he was selected to coach the U.S. Olympic team more than once. His reign over basketball ran from 1930 to 1972.

Tony Hinkle of Butler University in Indianapolis, Indiana, was a winning coach who knew how to select and mold players into teams. His teams played AAU opponents with great success from the 1920s to the 1960s.

Branch McCracken's teams at Indiana University won two NCAA titles (1940 and 1953) and used the fast break effectively. He coached a number of outstanding players, including Bob Leonard, Walt Bellamy, and Don Schlundt.

At the University of California, Pete Newell's team won an NCAA crown in 1960 with precise techniques that revolved beautifully around center play. Coaches still use some of his concepts today. John Wooden won more NCAA titles (10) than any other coach, and also used the press extremely well.

Many of the New York Celtic players became great coaches. They were not only superb strategists, but they could demonstrate to players how to perform skills at higher levels.

CHAPTER 3

Applications of Physical Principles

There are certain physical or mechanical principles that govern the actions of all creatures on the earth. Factors such as friction, temperature, gravity and resistance to it, clothing, floor resilience, and physical condition affect player performance. Players and coaches must understand how to combat or use these physical realities to gain individual efficiency and team advantages.

Some of the terms used here are technical. They will be explained as simply as possible in basketball terminology and applied in performance situations. Some are simplified for easier understanding.

Mechanics is the branch of physics dealing with motion or forces causing motion. Mechanics is concerned with the effects of forces on objects and includes statics (bodies at rest or forces in equilibrium) and kinetics (forces producing or modifying motion). In basketball, mechanics involves the force imparted against the ball by a player in throwing, and this force in turn is affected by the methods of executing throwing skills. This term is used in explaining some of the remainder of the definitions, which are presented alphabetically.

Acceleration is a term applied to the rate at which the velocity of a body increases or decreases per unit of time. It may be negative or positive. When the velocity is constant, the acceleration is zero.

Basketball players often run down the court, trying to go faster and faster. However, a player approaching the basket or attempting to pass must be under control. It is hard to make a layup or stay within boundaries at top speed. Scientists have determined that human beings are poor

33

judges of others' velocities. Consequently, the ability to vary velocity quickly is an asset in both offensive and defensive situations.

The very slow offensive player may be able to elude a defensive player by varying speed. Conversely, while a defensive player may appear slow, he or she may concentrate on quick initial movements to offset slow running speeds.

Angle of incidence and angle of reflection are the striking and rebounding angles of a ball (object) contacting the backboard or the floor (another object or surface). If the two objects come in contact with one another in a perpendicular impact, there is no friction, because friction occurs parallel to the floor. This is the only time this is true. If the impact is not perpendicular to the floor, then the force of friction changes the rebound angle so that the horizontal component of the rebound is reduced. If there is any spin on the ball, this modification is a bit more complicated.

The angle of incidence is equal to the angle of reflection only when the ball is thrown against the glass in a near perpendicular line, as is sometimes done by a high jumping player close to the front of the basket. The ball will rebound directly forward, and gravity will bring it down onto the court. However, if the ball hits the glass at an angle (oblique angle of incidence), the angle of incidence will be different from the angle of reflection because the vertical velocity is affected by the coefficient of restitution and the horizontal velocity is affected by friction (Figure 3–1 and 3–2).

(backboard)

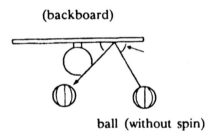

ball (without spin)

Figure 3–1A. Effect of elasiticity will reduce angle of rebound very slightly.

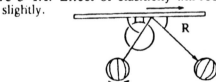

Figure 3–1B. Horizontal velocity of rebound is greater due to friction caused by spin.

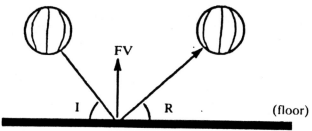

Figure 3-1C. Ball with no spin contacting floor.

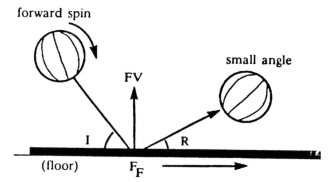

Figure 3-1D. This is due to effects of elasticity plus increase in horizontal velocity due to friction caused by spin.

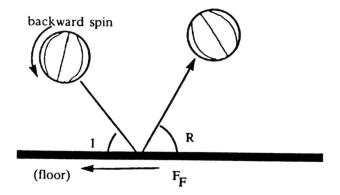

Figure 3-1E. Greater angle due to effects of elasticity which tends to reduce vertical velocity and decrease horizontal velocity due to friction caused by spin.

35

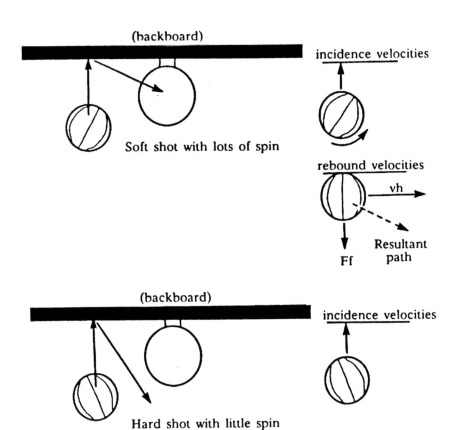

(backboard)

incidence velocities

Soft shot with lots of spin

rebound velocities

vh

Ff   Resultant
      path

(backboard)

incidence velocities

Hard shot with little spin

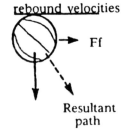

rebound velocities

Ff

Resultant
path

Figure 3–2.

A layup is made very close to the basket. It involves both side spin (which is dominant) and back spin. The back spin reduces the velocity of the ball. The side spin then takes over, causing the ball to rebound down into the basket (Figure 3-3).

Usually the angle of reflection is the lesser of the two angles, and this makes it easier to rebound or tip in the rebounding ball because its angle in reflection is higher, particularly with a soft backward spin.

A ball that is thrown from one side of the basket and misses, but goes high enough on the board to have a chance to go through the basket, will rebound to the opposite side more than 50 percent of the time. Players know this and try to station themselves in the best positions for catching.

(backboard)

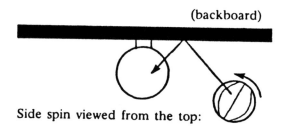

Side spin viewed from the top:

(backboard)

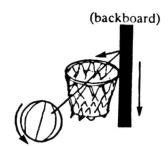

Figure 3-3.

Back spin seen from the side:

Attenuation involves reducing or absorbing force or energy. Basketball players who have "good hands" can catch a ball, even though the velocity varies, by attenuating the force. The ball is gradually, not abruptly decelerated. Players who have not acquired this ability frequently drop the ball and are said to have "board hands."

Braking force is a force that decelerates the body or a segment thereof. It is applied to retard or arrest a motion. A basketball player's foot is placed so that the forward velocity of the body is slowed or stopped by the muscular force created in pushing on the floor. The body is lowered and moved backward from a wide, staggered stance. The reaction force of the floor and friction slow the player. In essence, the player pushes against the floor and the floor pushes back against the body. It works better when the body is low, because the force is closer to the center of gravity. A player must push hard against the floor and avoid leaning too far forward or to either side. If the velocity is not great, the player may be able to stop abruptly from an upright position or change direction without difficulty.

Center of gravity is that imaginary point at which the body is in balance. It is the intersection of the three cardinal planes: the sagittal plane, which is the vertical plane that divides the body into two equally balanced right and left sections; the transverse plane, which divides the body into upper and lower sections; and the frontal plane, which divides the body into front and rear sections (Figure 3–4). If an airborne body rotates, it revolves around its center of gravity.

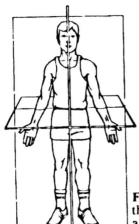

Figure 3–4. The center of gravity is where the three planes intercept. Adapted from Cooper and Glassaw, *Kinesiology*, p.34

The center of gravity is located at about 57 percent of a male's standing height, measuring from the soles of his feet. In the female, it is at about 54 percent of her total height. The center of gravity is at about the level of the second sacral section of the vertebral column and more toward the back of the body. It changes with any change in body position.

A basketball guard must continuously estimate the location of the center of gravity in his opponent (Figure 3-5). The belt buckle area is a good landmark. If a guard's attention is focused on this area, extraneous moves such as fakes should not cause him or her to move into the air or sideways prematurely. A player who is guarding from the rear uses peripheral vision to watch the second sacral segment level of the offensive player's body to avoid being faked.

Figure 3-5. The approximate location of the center of gravity of the offensive and defensive player is shown here. The offensive player has caused the defensive player to shift the center of gravity too far to the right, thus enabling the offensive player to dribble by him. From Cooper and Siedentop.

If an offensive player is quick and frequently drives around a defensive player, the defensive player should move the legs into a staggered position, lowering the center of gravity and widening the base of support. If the offensive player is not a strong outside shooter, the defensive player can also move farther away.

A tall center often has trouble guarding a small, quick guard. The rapid mobility of the smaller player is due partially to a lower center of gravity and a greater ability to initiate action quickly. Conversely, a coach will ask a taller offensive player to "post up" or move under the basket on a shorter player, since the taller individual has a higher center of gravity and can catch and pass the ball at greater heights.

Centripetal force is found in all rotary movements and is a constant force directed toward the center. The equal and opposite partner force is referred to as *Centrifugal force* or "center fleeing force." These forces are important when a body is moving in a curved path.

During certain situations, a basketball player moves in a curved path by creating centripetal force against the floor directed inward toward the center of the curve. A lean toward the center while moving forward helps in executing a turn by directing the applied forces toward the center. A player may move the outside foot to a wide base and push outward. Ground friction is directed in to turn the player.

The most notable example of the use of centripetal force is when a guard or forward cuts around a center to receive a pass by running in a curved path. The guard pushes against the floor with the outside foot and leans in, the degree depending on the speed. In most instances the cut is started a short distance away so the guard can actually set into the curve without slowing down. The guard's center of gravity is lowered in short turns. It is possible for a player to be going so fast that sharp turns are difficult. It may be impossible to push hard enough against the ground for enough centripetal force to cut. However, in most situations a guard controls the move into the curve and then accelerates.

Coefficient of restitution is the quantification of elasticity (the property of elastic bodies that cause them to regain their original shapes after compression). When a basketball is thrown against the backboard or bounced on the floor, both the ball and the contacted surface are compressed, if ever so slightly. There is a way of determining the coefficient of restitution of the ball. It is the extent to which a ball dropped to the floor regains a percentage of its original height. It is found by measuring the perpendicular height to which it returns on rebound from the floor. Hay (5, p.80) has shown that an official basketball has a coefficient of restitution of about .76. This will vary according to ball surfaces and temperatures. The coefficient of restitution of 1.0 would be the theoretical maximum number, but it can never be attained in actuality.

Normally, basketballs used in games are inflated to specific pressures stamped on the balls. The ball is tested by dropping it from a height of six feet. If it bounces approximately 75 percent of six feet (4.5 feet), it is considered live and playable.

Certain individuals have been known to pump up a ball to a pressure exceeding the recommended amount, making the ball surface very tight. If this condition goes undetected by the officials and coaches, the ball will bounce higher and rebound faster, causing the players great difficulty.

Sometimes the playing surface has "dead" spots or places where the floor is too elastic and "takes up" the bounce of the ball. The ball will rebound poorly and will be difficult to dribble.

Gymnasium floors and basketballs are much more lively warm than cold. In the cold, molecules of air in the floor contract, reducing bounce. The reverse is true if the floors are warm. As a youngster, I played outdoors with an inflated rubber ball. Periodically my friends and I would go inside to warm the ball over a stove. The expanded air made the ball lively enough to dribble again.

Force couple is a pair of equal forces acting in opposite directions along parallel lines. A force couple produces a torque (turning force) on an object with no net force. In other words, a basketball will rotate but not move linearly. Most spins of a ball, produced by one or both hands and the floor, are rotations caused by a force couple.

A pivot by a basketball player is the result of the application of a force couple. A torque is produced as the player rotates about on one foot without moving it off the floor (Figure 3-6). The pivot resembles a revolving door with torque produced as the player spins away from his opponent. An equal and opposite force to the pivoting force is applied by the grounded foot. There is zero net force to cause linear motion.

Friction is resistance to motion due to the contact of two surfaces moving relative to each other. It is a force which opposes every effort to slide or roll one body over another. It always occurs parallel to the two surfaces. It may be a hindrance or an asset for basketball players.

Figure 3-6. The basketball pivot.

In general, friction does not depend on velocity. Rather, it depends on the load and on the nature and conditions of the rubbing surfaces. Starting friction is distinctly greater than sliding friction. A player will encounter greater friction in starting than in moving. Friction usually decreases with increasing speed. This is why a very fast player must slow down to create enough traction to stop or change direction without slipping (Figure 3-7).

Figure 3-7. To stop after a run, this player would need to lower the center of gravity if the velocity is high, to increase the stopping area and to utilize better friction. The ground reaction forces and friction forces as to their direction of application are depicted.

If two surfaces rubbing together offer resistance when sliding, then large horizontal or frictional forces can be generated without slipping. This would allow a player with high velocity in one direction to apply large deceleration forces without stopping.

In basketball, the nature of the sole shoe and floor can vary from court to court. Tartan floors grip rubber soled basketball shoes very well. Sweat and dirt on wood playing surfaces lower frictional forces, often causing slippage. When the grip between the shoe sole and playing surface is too great, the knee may be injured when a player attempts to change direction. Basically, the ligaments stretch or tear when lateral shearing forces are great. This can happen when the foot is fixed. Coaches must become familiar with playing floors and possibly have more than one type of shoe available for players. The ground reaction force vector pushes the player into the air, and a frictional force pushes the player horizontally.

Friction is reduced when the surfaces moving across one another are smooth and hard. A wet surface offers less friction than a dry one, so attendants must wipe off perspiration or liquids from court floors. Players need traction (friction) to avoid slipping.

Often a player wants to increase friction by using shoe soles with indentations or small incomplete holes to modify the surface. The increased friction enables the player to stop quickly and, with sufficient force exerted by the legs through the feet, to move again rapidly.

Basketball shoes often have a set of circular rings on the ball of the shoe sole. This configuration allows the shoe to slip during turning, but keeps the shoe firm during starting and stopping.

Basketball players, particularly in high school, sometimes have to practice or play on a floor that has been covered with wax for a dance. Friction is reduced, and players have to take short, slower steps and keep their feet under their centers of gravity. When slippage is too great, players have to remain upright to maintain balance.

Rolling friction is weaker than sliding friction, but it can have a great impact on a basketball contacting the floor or the backboard. On impact, the spinning ball is deformed, creating friction. Some players can spin the ball enough so that when it strikes high on the backboard, it deflects down into the basket. If a ball is spinning at the moment it strikes the floor or backboard, the velocity and direction of the ball will be changed in accordance with the original velocity and amount of spin.

A ball can be thrown with either back spin or top spin, both of which alter the speed of movement after impact. A ball thrown with top spin against the floor will bounce rapidly forward toward a teammate. One with backspin will, because of greater friction since the spin is opposite to the friction force, tend to move upward. A player must often move forward to catch it and prevent the opponent from interfering with the catch.

Gravity is a force that objects experience while on earth or in the air. It is a constant, downward acceleration. Any attempt to move directly upward requires muscular force, which is opposed by gravity. The pull or acceleration of gravity varies slightly at different locations on the earth, but essentially it is constant.

Bodies are attracted to the earth with a force of approximately 9.8 meters/second2 Limitations on the upward movement of a basketball player are determined by the relationship of body weight to the force that the muscles, through the feet, can produce, as well as the speed at which this force is produced (force x time = impulse).

The player who leans forward has the help of gravity to initiate starting movements in running. The runner actually falls, then recovers with the feet.

In the jump, the player must work against gravity, creating a pushing force against the floor through the legs and feet and quickly propelling the body upward. The slower player with a large body mass and less forceful muscular contractions will not jump very high. A high leaping player overcomes the force of gravity upon leaving the floor, but gravity slows his upward velocity eventually to zero, and the player begins to descend at an acceleration of 9.8 meters/second2 When the player contacts the floor again, his speed is equal to the takeoff speed. Such a player must learn to land gently to avoid injury and return to action quickly.

Impulse is the product of a force and the time over which it acts (force x time = impulse). A player going in for a dunk creates a force against the floor through the feet in preparation for the takeoff. It takes a certain amount of time to apply this force. Those who leap the highest create the greatest impulses relative to their masses. However, the best jumpers create large impulses through the application of large forces for very short periods. This phenomenon has been measured by a force plate. Contrary to popular belief, the time on the force plate was less and the impulse greater for those leaping the highest.

Levers are present in human beings as the main means of movement. Bones are levers that rotate at joints by means of muscles and external forces. The muscle attachments are located at particular sites on the bones for effective movement.

A lever is able to do work when energy is transmitted through it. Energy is derived from muscular contractions and is transmitted by the bones of the body to move body segments such as the arms. The movement of these segments can transmit energy to an external object such as a basketball.

Basketball players use their arms, legs, and bodies as levers while playing. Parts of a lever include: 1) the fulcrum, or axis of rotation of the bone; 2) the site of the attachment of the muscles; and 3) the location of the center of gravity in the player's arm, often including the weight of the ball. All of these constitute resistance to movement.

The three basic types of levers are first class, second class, and third class. The majority of levers in the human body are third class. Typical anatomical levers are displayed in Figure 3-8. In third class levers, the distance from the effort arm to the fulcrum is small. Consequently, the system favors speed and manipulation over strength.

Class of lever

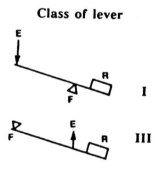

Three classes of levers

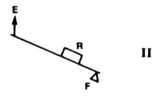

Figure 3-8. Three classes of levers from Cooper and Glassow Kinesiology, Fourth Edition, p 33.

What do levers have to do with basketball performance? A player who possesses the ball needs to pull it close to his body to decrease the resistance arm. The effort side of the lever is stronger. The player who wishes to throw the basketball a long distance would need to extend the throwing arm as much as possible to increase the length of the lever (Figure 3–9). This gives a good range of motion at the end of the lever where the ball is being held, but it requires stronger muscular force to overcome the extra resistance. There is an advantage if a player is sufficiently strong and has long limbs (long levers).

Figure 3–9. Preparatory action of triceps brachii in forearm extension in shooting. Note the impending leverage action. This is a first class lever.

The position of the leg muscles on the bones of top runners and jumpers favors good leverage. Usually, in excellent jumpers, the gastrocnemius and soleus muscles in the calf are located closer to the knee joint in the rear of the leg than they are in weaker jumpers. Speed runners possess heavy quadriceps and hamstring muscles in the upper parts of their thighs. These are often much larger than the muscles of the lower legs in slower runners. The large muscles' proximity to the axis of rotation (the hip) and the smaller muscles' longer distance away illustrates the leverage advantage. The slower runner with large lower leg muscles has a disadvantage in leverage.

Mass is the measure of expression of the inertia of a body or its reluctance to change its motion. It is the amount of matter contained in a body. The larger the mass of an object, the less acceleration it will have when acted upon by a given force. Mass is constant and involves resistance to change of motion. (See also Weight.)

Momentum is the quality of motion in a body as measured by the product of its mass and velocity (mass x velocity = momentum). If two players of similar height are racing down the court at the same velocity, then the one with the greater mass has the greater momentum. If a collision occurs, the player with the greater mass should have more effect on the direction and speed of the resulting movement.

Sir Isaac Newton formulated *three laws of motion: the law of inertia, the law of acceleration, and the law of interaction.*

The law of inertia states that "a body at rest or in motion continues at rest or in straight line direction unless acted upon by an external force." To initiate movement, a player, regardless of external forces, must first overcome the inertia of his or her own body. Body posture resembles that of an upright sprinter using the force of the legs against the floor for a quick start.

A basketball player who is holding position or moving in one direction while guarding will be affected by a push or strike from an opponent. The external force may cause movement or a change in direction. Usually the opponent will be called for a foul.

The legitimacy of a situation in which a player holds position and takes a "charge" from an opponent who is driving to the basket often can be determined if the offended player's body is driven back as a whole. If the defender falls over in body parts, rather than as a total entity, the defender is acting and no true charge has occurred. However, no blocking foul should be assessed, provided the defender is planted and makes no movement toward the offensive player.

The law of acceleration states that "the motion of a body is directly related to the force acting on it and is inversely related to its mass." The rate of change of momentum or the acceleration of a body having constant mass is proportional to the force acting on it and occurs in the direction in which the force acts. If a basketball player deflects the ball with the hand in a pass or in a rebound, the ball will move in a direction that results from the original flight path, the speed of the ball, and the direction of the hand. This is called the resultant. Batted or deflected balls sometimes travel in unusual directions.

If a player grabs an opponent while running down the court, the opponent's acceleration usually is reduced, as is that of the original player. The opponent's mass added to that of the original player's reduces acceleration.

The law of interaction or action–reaction states that "for every action there is an equal and opposite reaction." If a player is running down the court and pushes with the feet against the floor, force is created against the player in a backward direction. In turn, the player is moved forward as a result of the resistance (or force) exerted by the floor against the feet. The more force exerted by the feet, the more the floor exerts a force in the opposite direction.

There are many other examples in basketball where the ball or the hand of a player exerts a force against some object and receives a force exerted in the opposite direction. Probably the most notable example is when a player shoots the ball with great force against the backboard. The backboard, in turn, exerts a large force against the ball, causing it to rebound so forcefully that the player rebounding cannot attenuate the force and catch the ball. (One unscrupulous coach had the backboard and basket tightened on the day of a home game so that the ball would rebound harder and faster than the opponents anticipated. This helped his team neutralize the advantage of the opposing team's tall center.)

A careless dribbler sometimes pushes the ball against the floor with too much force, and the floor in turn exerts too much force against the ball. The player may fumble the ball or be called for traveling.

Power is the work done per unit of time (work/time). A basketball player in a jump is doing work in a given time. Those who jump the highest perform more work in the same time, or do the same work in less time. Power is related to speed and is important in understanding why speed is essential in sports. In basketball, a player with great speed converts the velocity into vertical thrust in jumping and may go much higher than a player with low velocity.

Strength is the ability to move an object of increased weight over a certain distance or a given weight over a greater distance (work/distance). When two players grasp a basketball at the same time, the stronger player should secure possession. A player with great strength, however, may find that use of better leverage by a weaker player offsets any advantage.

Trajectory is the path of an object moving in space. A ball thrown into the air will rapidly move upward until its velocity is zero. The velocity at release is equal to the velocity at landing at the same height of the release. The ball travels a curved parabolic path. The horizontal and vertical displacements depend on the angle and speed of the ball at takeoff. When a basketball is launched toward the basket, the speed and angle of release will determine the distance it will travel. A player who wants to shoot at a higher angle than usual may reduce the speed of release and the distance. A low angle of release ordinarily means the ball is traveling too fast to go in the basket. A small player driving toward the basket and confronted by a taller player will raise the angle of release to avoid having the shot blocked.

When velocity is constant, as the angle of release is increased, the distance the object moves in displacement increases as well, up to a release angle of approximately 42 to 43 degrees. In mathematical terms, a theoretical angle to use for distance to be gained from a throw is about 43 degrees from a player in a set position. Any release above or below that theoretical angle with a constant speed should result in diminished distance. A ball held at 7 feet from the basket should be released with control speed at an angle of 46 to 55 degrees. When the ball is very near or above the basket, a higher angle, up to about 90 degrees, can be used. Hudson (6) found the proper angle of release in a free throw to be about 62 degrees.

Of course, the standing height of a player will affect the angle of release. The very tall player often releases the ball from a higher position and perhaps releases at a greater velocity because of a longer throwing arm (See Lever) and faster arm and hand speed.

The speed of release is an important factor in an offensive player's ability to elude a defensive player while shooting. Yet, a ball released with great velocity may rebound with too much speed to be easily caught. A missed three-point shot rebounds farther than a two-point shot. A good scorer usually has a quick release and a soft touch. Players also try to release the ball with a backward spin so that it rebounds down. Friction aids in reducing vertical rebound velocity.

Gravity will oppose the vertical movement of a ball or person propelled into the air at an angle greater than zero. Horizontal velocity will be constant, regardless of air resistance, but vertical velocity varies because of acceleration due to gravity. A person jumping either forward or backward in space will move both vertically and horizontally. The vertical impulse at takeoff will determine the height of the jump (force x time). The angle of takeoff is a factor in determining the horizontal distance from takeoff to landing. Most jump shooters try to jump as vertically as possible.

While an angle of approximately 45 degrees is theoretically necessary for maximal distance for a released object (when landing and release are at the same height), this is not necessarily the best angle in modern basketball shooting. A player is usually within 15 to 20 feet of the basket, and the ball may be released near or above the level of the basket height. A slam dunk, where the ball is elevated directly above the basket, is the simplest way to score (Figure 3–10). It obviously favors the taller or high jumping player. The farther away the ball is launched from the basket, the more arch is needed for the best descent to the basket. If the angle of release is above or below 46 to 55 degrees, up to 62 degrees, the ball may travel less distance and be too short, too long, or too flat.

Figure 3–10. The dunk.

As soon as a player pushes the ball up vertically to get more height in the shot, the horizontal release speed imparted to the ball is reduced. The result is a short shot or an uncontrolled shot that may not be propelled in the proper direction.

Translation or linear motion is accomplished when a body and all its parts move in the same direction at the same time. It is motion in a line, even though the line is not necessarily straight. There is rotary as well as linear movement in most actions, which classifies them as general, even though the result is linear in nature.

Rotary movement occurs when a body rotates about a point or axis. This rotary motion is combined with linear motion in most activities. The body of a player in the air could be represented by the center of gravity and such body parts as the hands rotating about an axis.

The segments of the lower extremities rotate about the joints to project the body into the air. Many of a player's movements on the court are combinations of linear (often curvilinear motion) and angular motion. The actions must be studied as two motions, rather than as one.

A thrown basketball rotates about some point in space as it moves along a curved path. The ball, if it is spinning, also revolves around its axis of rotation.

A player who rotates in the air must initiate the turning action prior to leaving the ground by moving one foot, the arms, the head and the trunk in the direction of the desired rotation. There isn't enough time in the air to accomplish this action. The arms are often used in the turn by keeping them as close to the body as possible once the player is airborne. If the player has possession of the ball, he or she may have to keep it away from an opponent during the turn. Upon completing the turn in the air, the player may attempt to shoot or pass.

Vector is a line representing a physical quantity that has magnitude and direction in space, such as velocity, acceleration, and force. It is distinguished from scalar, which represents only magnitude. A jump shooter imparts a certain velocity to the ball in a given direction toward the basket at a certain angle (Figure 3–11). Usually the ball is spinning backward when it is released. The velocity at release may be represented by a vector. Control of magnitude and direction is essential to a good shooter.

Figure 3–11. The velocity of the ball at release is represented by a vector.

Weight is the measure of the force with which bodies tend to be pulled toward the earth's center, or it is the quality thus measured. The weight of a basketball player is a quotient of the player's mass and the acceleration due to the pull of gravity. It varies only slightly according to the player's location on earth. (The weight of the body is slightly lower at the equator, slightly higher in the northern hemisphere. Mass, however, is constant. (See also Mass in this chapter.)

CHAPTER 4

Analyses of Fundamental Basketball Skills

The principles and supporting statements in this chapter are derived from both qualitative and quantitative information. Technical terminology is held to a minimum. Analyses of the skills are presented in alphabetical order.

BALL HANDLING

Ball handling combines several skills: dribbling, passing, and receiving. Most experts think these combined skills are best taught through drills. Newton emphasized three main things in developing good ball handlers: fingertip control, quickness of hands in manipulating the ball, and use of both hands, alternately (10, p. 27).

Newton considered ball handling the easiest of all basketball skills to learn and shooting the most difficult. Such actions as spinning the ball on one finger and rotating the ball over the back of the hand, down the arm, across the back, and down the back of the other arm give young players confidence. They should also learn to lie on their backs in a supine or in a side lying position, dribbling continuously, then rise and move back down the floor without losing contact with the ball.

Being able to dribble the ball without seeing it, pass the ball without looking at the receiver, and catch the ball without stabbing are sound ball handling techniques. Players must have a "feel" for the ball. Even catching the ball behind the back is valuable as a learning tool.

Volleyball skills such as setting and passing the ball to a setter are practical maneuvers to use in teaching ball handling. Adult players should use basketballs during these practices and watch for injuries caused by the larger, heavier balls. Children may use volleyballs, since it is easier to get a "feel" for smaller balls.

Women use smaller balls in NCAA competition, making ball handling, passing, and shooting somewhat easier.

CATCHING

Catching, which includes both receiving a pass and intercepting an opponent's pass, involves ball handling. Cousy states that, "The way a pass is caught is determined by such factors as the flight path and velocity of the ball, the movement of the receiver, the proximity of defensive players, and the kind of offensive moves to be made with the ball after it is caught." (5)

Both passer and receiver are responsible for a successful catch. If a receiver bobbles, fumbles, or drops the ball, it may be his or her error. But if the passer throws the ball too hard, too long, too low, or out of reach, the passer is at fault. Cooper and Siedentop have listed a number of principles of performance in catching a basketball.

1. "Whenever possible the ball should be caught out in front of the upper part of the receiver's body." The receiver may have to move forward to receive the ball to elude an opponent who is guarding closely.

2. "The gradual dissipation (attenuation) of the force (velocity) of a thrown ball is primarily accomplished by 'giving' with the hands as the ball is received." In some instances, this is accomplished with flexion of the elbow, a backward movement of the upper torso, and in rare instances, a step backward.

The recoil as the ball contacts the receiver's hands is not severe, but there is necessarily absorption of the kinetic energy of the moving ball or else the ball is dropped. The force is absorbed by the fingers, hands, arms, and sometimes the body. The slightest movement of the head or other parts of the body may cause a shift of the center of gravity. The flight path of the ball may not be tracked correctly or the receiver may fail to recognize the intended flight path. The movement of the passer's hands will be out of direct alignment with the ongoing ball.

3. "The receiver should never take the eyes off of the ball in flight." A basketball, because of its size and relatively low velocity, should be

easy to catch. The receiver should visually trace the ball in flight as directly as possible. To say the ball is seen into the hands is good teaching and practice, but it is not actually possible, since the eyes see in short spurts. Viewing the ball out of the corner of the eyes is not recommended. Peripheral vision is effective only to identify the location of the ball, not to trace a flight path. The gaze must be steady and direct.

4. "The hands should be in a near thumbs–together position with the fingers pointing upward to receive a pass thrown above the waist." This is done so the ball will land in the cup of the hands and then be grasped by the fingers. A ball caught by the fingers alone may be dropped or knocked away.

5. "The hands should be in a little–fingers–together position to receive a pass that is thrown below the waist." This is done so that the cup of the hands is facing the flight of the ball. The receiver may need to adjust hands and body position as the ball nears. The passer is only accurate within a few inches at best. The receiver tries to make the passer's task easier by setting a target that is as stationary as possible with the hands.

6. "When closely guarded, the receiver should catch the ball with the palm of one hand under and the palm of the other on top of the ball." This grip enables the offensive player to withstand more easily the force of a slap or to move the ball away from the direction of a slap (Figure 4–1).

Figure 4-1. One hand under, one hand on top catching position.

7. A long high pass to a target beyond a receiver must be caught over the shoulder with the little fingers together and the palms up and facing the rear. This is similar to a wide receiver's catch in football. The attenuation of the ball takes place as the arms move up and out on contact to an extended waist–high arms position (Figure 4–2).

Figure 4-2. Over the shoulder catching position.

8. When a pass is made to a receiver who is very close to a defensive player, the receiver may receive the ball temporarily with one or two hands but immediately push the ball away from the opponent in a kind of dribble, letting the ball contact the floor and then retrieving it. The receiver may need to move toward the ball in catching to avoid a guard. If a ball is caught with one hand, the player should immediately use the second hand for grasping.

A player's position on the floor sometimes dictates catching posture. For example, the pivot player must be moving toward the ball or have a defensive player clearly behind. If the defensive player is on one side or the other, the offensive player must move toward the ball or maintain a stance to prevent the defensive player from moving into the ball's path. The pivot player must set a target, perhaps by raising both arms, so the passer knows where to throw the ball. The pivot's stance, if stationary, is to flex the knees, protrude the buttocks, and maintain an upright trunk. This is called a "sitting position."

If a defensive play fronts the pivot, the pivot should raise one hand to indicate contact, and the ball should be lobbed over the head of the defensive player. The pivot must avoid pushing the defensive player first when the ball is in flight. Slight contact of the two players, however, could stop or change the direction of the defensive player and help the pivot move toward the basket.

Other offensive players, such as the guards, usually turn their bodies toward the flight path of the ball, but may at times receive the ball as the pivot does, even though they are away from the basket. Guards and forwards may have to step in front of their defensive players to catch the ball unmolested. They may need to assume a sitting position as the pivot does.

The passer must know which passes teammates can handle. Passers should not throw an "alley oop" pass to a poor jumper, unless he or she is very tall. A slow–moving receiver needs accurate passes. A quick runner may want a passer to lead for a cut or a backdoor move. Tall players have trouble catching low passes because they have high centers of gravity and prefer being upright to receiving in low positions.

Receivers with small hands need soft, accurate passes. Players with large hands, however, can receive with one hand and often retrieve balls that were thrown inaccurately. Players with "board hands" need soft passes also. Fast passes to receivers who cannot attenuate the force may result in turnovers.

DRIBBLING

From a teaching and learning perspective, dribbling is the first, and maybe one of the most important skills that a young player should master (4, p. 31). Dribbling, with good ball handling, makes other skills easier to perfect.

In order for a player to move up and down the court effectively, without passing, dribbling is essential. Hay stated that "the objective in dribbling is to advance the ball when passing is impossible or less desirable." (8, p. 213)

A good shooter who is not a good dribbler and ball handler, plays with a handicap. For example, a center who receives the ball in the back court as a safety valve and finds no unguarded teammate may be forced to dribble into the offensive end of the court. A player who is unable to dribble well may lose possession.

The dribbler applies force to the ball often in a forward and downward direction. The floor, in turn, exerts force against the ball, causing it to bounce upward. The height of the return bounce depends on the force exerted by the dribbler as the ball leaves the hands, the type of floor, and the air inflation pressure of the ball.

If the player is moving as the dribbling takes place, the ball will follow a curved path until it contacts the floor and rebounds at a forward angle. Just prior to release, the ball takes on the momentum of the dribbler. If dropped at this point, the ball will not fall directly downward (perpendicular), but will fall to the floor in front of the dribbler.

Cooper and Siedentop (4, p. 31) stated that "dribbling at a high level is a kinesthetic and tactile skill." Cousy believes the three most important aspects of dribbling are "posture, ball control, and field of vision." (5, p. 80)

There are other important facts about dribbling.

1. The dribbler must be able to use either hand effectively.

2. A high dribble involves a greater amount of wrist flexion–extension than a low dribble.

3. The low dribble is controlled, with the upper body in a flexed and sometimes near upright position, the hips and knees flexed. This puts the dribbler closer to the ball and enables protection to be more effective.

4. The good dribbler keeps the upper torso in different degrees of flexion and the head and neck upright in order to see defensive players and teammates. Peripheral vision is important. A dribbler may be able to see 180 degrees in either direction from the sides and the entire court by rotating the head.

5. In the low dribble and in certain other dribbling situations, the body of the dribbler must be between the defensive player and the ball for protection purposes.

6. The faster the dribble is executed, the higher the dribbler's center of gravity. To run at controlled, high speeds, the dribbler's body is upright. A low center of gravity in dribbling, however, enables the player to change direction quickly.

7. Normally there is one step with each dribble, but there may be more steps as the dribbler's speed increases. At high speeds, the ball is pushed out in front more forcefully and has a lower angle of contact with the floor (Figure 4–3).

Figure 4-3. Speed dribbler. Since the ball is in front, indicates it has taken on the momentum of the moving dribbler.

8. Every dribbler needs the ability to change direction. In the behind-the-back dribble, the defensive player moves in one direction to stop the dribbler, only to find that the dribbler has moved laterally in a new direction.

9. Control of the ball while dribbling is essential. The fingers are key, although the wrist, elbow, and entire arm are at times involved. The action of these joints controls the height and speed of the ball. The four fingers (digits) of the dribbling hand contact the ball – the thumb should not be involved. The wrist and fingers extend and flex. The ball, after contacting the floor, bounces and comes to rest momentarily against the palm of the pronated hand (Figure 4-4).

Figure 4-4. Ball rests briefly in palm of hand. This dribbler is moving on a curve.

GUARDING

It is difficult to separate individual defense movements into a single category called guarding. Defense should be team-oriented, not individualistic. The most exacting so-called individual defense is played man-to-man. Zone defense can be individualistic to a degree, but it is less precise, less demanding, and not as clearly delineated as to individual responsibility. It is not as easy in a zone defense to pinpoint accountability as it is in man-to-man. The mechanics of action in man-to-man are more easily recognized and definable, so this discussion focuses primarily on man-to-man. Cooper and Siedentop listed a number of principles of individual defense (4, p. 107, 108). Other principles have been added here.

1. "Playing good defense in a competitive situation is more often a matter of attitude, desire, and concentration than it is proper execution of skills." While mastery of the mechanics of defensive play is essential, motivation is the key to an inspired defensive effort. Sometimes great offensive players neglect defense. Trading baskets in a game benefits no one.

60

2. "The main purpose of individual defense is to contain (the player) who has the ball and to prevent (the player) on the offensive team from scoring."

Figure 4-5.
Parallel foot stance.

Figure 4-6.
Stride stance.

Figure 4-7.
Fencer's stance.

3. "Individual defense can be aided by the use of a mechanically sound stance." Each type of guarding stance has its advantages. A parallel foot stance is best used in guarding lateral movements (Figure 4-5). The stride stance is best to use against a cutting player, because the center of gravity is more toward the rear (Figure 4-6). A fencer's stance, with the rear foot turned sideward, gives the defensive player an opportunity for quick forward movements, since he or she may push with greater force against the floor (Figure 4-7). The fencer's stance, however, is not readily adaptable to lateral or backward movements. The stride position of the feet is the best all around stance. Generally, the most effective stance of a defensive player out on the court is "liable to attack." It is a compromise between being balanced and stable and being unstable enough to move quickly in any direction. Movements become a guessing game between opponents. To limit the offensive possibilities, a defensive player may try to force an offensive player to move in an undesirable path or to make a move too soon.

4. "Variations in defensive stance depend upon the immediate situation and the planned team strategy." It is possible to assume a defen-

sive stance in which the offensive player is overplayed to one side and cannot dribble or cut in a particular direction. Or, the defensive player may allow an opponent to head toward a location that is less desirable for the offense or where more defensive help is available.

5. "The use of proper eye focus and concentration are essential to being a good defensive player." The defensive player should focus on the offensive player's belt buckle area, especially when the offensive player is a cutter or a driver.

6. "The manner in which the first defensive stride (step) is taken as the offensive player moves and the angle of pursuit that is used are fundamental to displaying good defensive play."

7. "The footwork used by the defensive player should be continuously altered by the needs of the situation."

8. A defensive player should not leave the floor to block a shot until the offensive player is fully committed to jumping and shooting or passing. A player in the air cannot alter the flight pattern until he or she returns to the floor. The defensive player is almost helpless in the air. Some coaches will not permit their players to jump into the air to block a shot.

9. The arms of a defensive player are placed where a pass, shot, or dribble can best be countered. Both hands may be held high or low, or one hand may be high and the other low. There may be a constant change of arm positions. Zone players should keep both arms extended overhead to help close gaps in defense.

While playing against a non-cutter, both of the defensive player's hands may be held high. Playing against a dribbler-cutter requires the defensive player to keep both hands low.

Each change in arm position changes the location of the center of gravity and has its advantages and disadvantages. The ability to move the hands through a full range of arm movements without unduly altering the position of the center of gravity is essential to good guarding mechanics.

It is possible for a defensive player to "close the gap" and be very close to the offensive player. This may be disconcerting to the opponent, especially if the defensive player shifts the body to shut off a favored driving path. An offensive player can be forced to dribble with the non-preferred hand, and defensive player may stand directly in front of the preferred shooting hand. Clearly, defense should be considered in terms of the total body rather than just in terms of the position of the feet and arms. Some coaches like to force all offensive movements into a given direction, for example, the sidelines. This is done by overplaying one way and leaving the alternative open for easy movements.

Movement skills used in defensive play are not difficult to execute, yet some defensive players react slowly to clues made by offensive players. It may take slow-reacting players several years to learn to play individual defense intuitively. Yet, it is easier to learn defense than offense. Players may become reasonably good at defense after entering high school or even college.

Some college players who played inside positions in high school may be shifted to guard positions in college. The footwork and actions are different, especially since players travel both forward and backward. It is harder to keep up with opponents who travel greater distances.

Some players are quite capable on defense when they move forward or to the sides but have difficulty moving backward and guarding a cutting player. They are unable to shift their centers of gravity quickly enough in the rear direction to counteract the drive of the offensive players. When they move to the side or forward, their centers of gravity are projected accordingly. They may not be able to shift backward quickly, which leaves them vulnerable to offensive drives and cutting.

Some offensive moves are intended to begin with good defense that capitalizes on an opponent's mistakes. Effective defensive players cannot be immobilized. They must be able to take chances.

"The (defensive) stance must be a stable one so that a slight reaction (counteraction) by the defensive player to a 'false' (or fake) move by the offensive player will not throw the defensive player off balance. Increased stability (balance or equilibrium) is achieved by widening the base of support and lowering the center of gravity. Stability can be considered in direct proportion to the vertical and horizontal distance the center of gravity is from the base of support (feet). The feet (often in a stride position) are usually spread a distance just beyond the width of the shoulders (or even more, depending on the speed of the offensive player). The defensive player may assume a wide enough base to stop a speedster. The knees are flexed to an angle somewhere between 90 and 120 degrees." (4, p. 108-109)

Cooper and Siedentop also point out that "if the defender increases the angle of the knee flexion, thus lowering farther the center of gravity, the player would gain additional stability but at the expense of mobility." (4) In the lower position, the player is unable to raise the arms fast enough to defend against a jump shooter.

A good defensive player has to be careful not to shift the feet, particularly in a forward direction, just as the offensive player starts a drive for the basket. Recovery is not possible until the movement is complete – too late to stop the drive. If the foot of a defensive player is raised only a few centimeters off the floor in a slide, the player's center of gravity is so far forward that no movement can be made until the foot is firmly planted. Even leaning the body in response to a fake may leave the opposite side open for a movement by the offensive player.

In the past, there has been much discussion about the defensive player always using the slide step rather than a crossover step when moving on defense. This is effective when the defensive player is moving laterally a short distance. However, if an offensive player cuts quickly for the basket, the only way the defensive player can stay with the opponent is to use a crossover step and run, especially if a "back door" is taking place. In any situation that involves much distance, the crossover step is faster than the slide. However, when a player uses the crossover, the center of gravity is projected quite far in one direction. It may help to use the slide step in short, quick counter movements. It is to the defensive player's advantage to keep the feet as close to the floor as possible.

Teammates must notify a defensive player to offset a screen being set by one of the offensive players. The defensive player should be able to "feel" the offensive player coming up or across the floor to screen. The ability to continually shift the body to fight through a screen is necessary in a good defensive player.

When a defensive player guards an opponent who does not have the ball, he or she may maintain a certain distance from the offensive player on the court, all the time knowing the location of the ball. If possible, the ball should be kept in view, even by means of peripheral vision, which picks up movement more quickly than direct vision. If the defensive player has to choose between keeping the ball or the opponent in sight, the location of the ball is sacrificed in man–to–man. In a zone defense, the location of the ball is the top priority.

To knock the ball out of the hands of an offensive player, the defensive player normally uses the lead hand rather than the trail hand. To move the trail hand forward toward the ball causes the body to move a greater distance in one direction. Consequently, the defensive player may be out of position if the ball is missed. In most instances, a foul will occur. The hand movement should be up, not down, to knock the ball loose.

Guarding inside players is normally easier since they cover less distance. If an offensive player's back is to the basket, the defensive player guarding from behind should concentrate on a point near the belt line. If it starts to move up, shooting at the basket is the player's likely objective.

A defensive player guarding a much taller inside player must slide from side to side in line with the ball to prevent the taller player from receiving a pass. Playing behind such a player can be difficult, and help from teammates may be necessary. Sometimes two or three players sink back toward the taller player to prevent the taller player from receiving the ball. This is called a sagging defense.

The defensive player covering the inside player has the added responsibility of screening out to prevent offensive rebounding. A quick turn inside or a pivot into the path of the offensive rebounder should prevent an easy tip in. If an inside player moves out on the court, the defensive player follows normal principles of guarding. If an outside offensive player moves to the basket for a rebound, the defensive player first retreats and screens with a pivot. If the offensive player comes in full contact with the defensive player, deceleration takes place, and it is difficult for the offensive player to rebound.

JUMPING

Jumping is the act of projecting the body upward by exerting force through the feet. The feet push against the floor, and the floor "pushes back." The amount of "G" is often three to four times more than the body weight. (One "G" is the body weight at standing position.) If the upward thrust is not directed through the center of gravity, the jump will be off balance. Injury to the feet, legs, knees, or body may occur.

There are several types of jumps that a player can use. However, the emphasis here is on the vertical jump.

Before jumping, a player must know:
1. The necessary takeoff velocity.
2. The angle of projection, which depends on the desired outcome.
3. The force exerted against the floor and the amount of time the force is applied (force x time = impulse). The greater the impulse, the higher the jump.

A player is confronted with decisions that help determine type and style of jumping. Both offensive and defensive jumpers take readings of many factors and, by virtue of experience, intuitively respond.

A small, fast player may wish to gain height quickly to offset a high-jumping opponent. A high-jumper tries to maneuver for good position (under the basket, for example), and to jump before an opponent has created enough force to jump or block.

A poor jumper should estimate the rebound angle or path flight of the ball and attempt to be inside the opponent, under the basket, for a rebound. Poor jumping and slow feet may be offset by quick hands and good body position.

Increased takeoff velocity will result in a longer and/or higher jump. An offensive player may not want to jump as high as possible because of a defensive player's height or location, the positions of other players, and the distance of the ball from the basket. A shooter may decide not to drive and jump because of congestion. A defensive player may wait and jump to try and steal the ball or avoid jumping and try to steal if the rebounder brings the ball down and in toward the body.

Moving one arm up and the other forcefully down causes the raised arm to move higher (Figure 4-8). This is termed a diagonal and spiral movement of the trunk and elevated arm. This action causes the raised arm to move up as much as six additional inches. Even if the lower arm is not moved down forcefully, some three to four inches can be gained.

Figure 4-8. Leap for a tip-in or a center jump. Note the lower right arm and fully extended left arm. A player can reach farther with one arm than with two arms.

In some situations, the player will attempt to jump perpendicularly upward from a standing position. The feet should be no more than 10 inches apart. The knee should be flexed at a 115-degree angle for maximum lift. Great hip and knee extensor effort helps add height to the jump.

An initial downward swing of the arms adds force to the floor push.

arms ⬆

floor ⬇

force ⬇

The arms then move upward to catch or bat the ball away. The upward movement of the arms raises the player's center of gravity. A shooter brings the ball downward by flexing the arms and then elevates the ball in shooting.

The angle of takeoff from a standing position may be nearly vertical, depending on how the force is directed from the feet through the center of gravity. A slight lean in any direction at takeoff determines the ball's flight path. A displacement of the center of gravity during shooting may cause a missed shot.

A fade-away shooter may want a displacement to the rear at takeoff to elude a defensive player. The body is, in a sense, balanced, since the jumper prepares for such an action.

A vertical jump is measured by the difference between a standing hand reach and a hand reach from a vertical jump that was not preceded by a "crowhop" or a run. The highest height recorded by Chuck Williams was 28 inches for an entire conference (Table 4-1), which included black and white players (18, p. 43-45). Reports of vertical leaps of 44 to 48 inches seem exaggerated, unless the jumps followed runs.

A jump preceded by a run introduces additional factors, the most notable being the conversion of horizontal velocity into vertical lift. The height attained is greater than that achieved from a stationary starting position.

Table 4-1. Jumping height of 24 subjects, from Table 4, Chuck William's unpublished dissertation, p. 43. (Performers jumped from a non-running position.)

Subject number	Jumping height in inches
1	27
2	25
3	20
4	25
5	24
6	25
7	24
8	23
9	22
10	22
11	25
12	24
13	22
14	23
15	29
16	25
17	27
18	21
19	29
20	24
21	23
22	25
23	25
24	21

An offensive player attains a certain velocity heading toward the basket in preparation for a jump-rebound shot. The run must be fast enough for the player to attempt to outdistance the opponent, yet controlled enough to allow conversion of a horizontal run to an upward lift. If the offensive player runs too fast, it is impossible to jump effectively.

In the jump shot, the player uses a one-step method (see shooting section in this chapter). One foot is first planted, followed by the trailing foot. The feet, especially the one planted first, act as a braking force to partially decelerate the runner for a jump. Friction, caused by the bottom of the shoes rubbing against the floor, acts as a horizontal brake.

A defensive rebounder (Figure 4-9) must time the jump, note the location of the ball, and often box-out an offensive player. Reliable indicators of determination are good body

Figure 4-9. Defensive rebounder.

position and the sharp sound of the hands grasping the ball (Figure 4-10). The jumper-shooter must push firmly against the floor with a force that is strong and quick to gain elevation.

Figure 4-10. Rebounder has spread legs to prevent opponent from getting to the ball. He keeps the ball elevated to prevent a steal.

A jumper's center of gravity will tend to move forward as the player goes into the air. Both the center of gravity and the parabolic flight path of the player must be controlled. The parabola of the path of the center of gravity must be high and elevated, not long and low.

There is also a rotational component present in jump–run situations, since the player's center of gravity is usually in front of the base at take-off. This rotational aspect is overcome by moving the torso backward and jumping as near vertically as possible. The jump shooter's takeoff and landing angles should be similar, about 160 degrees.

The layup shot usually involves a run and a jump toward the basket. This should be more of a high jump than a long jump. The takeoff angle is 165 degrees. The jumper–shooter travels horizontally in the air for several feet. The path of the center of gravity is an elevated parabola.

In a driving layup situation, the player takes off on one foot. The next to the last stride should be longer and lower than the last stride to direct the jumper upward. The player going for a layup must jump more up than out.

PASSING

Cooper and Siedentop stated that "passing is the act of throwing the basketball from one player to another." (4, p. 38–39) The ball may be thrown the entire length of the court (baseball pass), it may be passed a few feet or yards (chest, overhead, and underhand shovel passes), or it may be passed only inches (handoff). Many opportunities to play good basketball are lost if some of the players are weak passers.

Passing the ball is one aspect of ball handling, and it is similar to throwing in other sports. The quicker the release of the ball, the less likely opposing team members are to intercept. Defensive players cannot move across, backward, or forward at the speed of a passed ball if it is thrown rapidly, accurately, and with deception.

Passing may be faster than dribbling, but poor passing can cause turnovers. On the other hand, a clever passer helps to set up openings that are otherwise unavailable. The play-making passer must be unselfish in every sense of the word. The open player is the passer's concern.

The fundamentals of passing must be practiced repeatedly so that they become automatic in all possible situations. A good passer is necessary for winning games and contributes to the performance potential of all teammates.

Allsen and Ruffner studied the relationship between the type of pass and turnovers. They identified the most frequent and effective passes in 72 games at the high school, college, and intramural levels (24 games in each level). The two-hand chest pass was used most frequently, almost 39 percent of the time. The one-hand baseball pass was used 19 percent of the time. The two-hand overhead pass followed at 16.6 percent. The one- and two-hand bounce passes finished last.

The one-hand baseball pass resulted in the lowest percentage of completion – 9.3 percent were lost to competition. The most successful passes were the two-hand chest passes and the two-hand shovel passes, which were lost only 2.5 percent of the time. The two-hand bounce pass was lost 7.3 percent of time, and the one-hand bounce pass, 9.1 percent. (1, 94, 105–107)

There is some merit to the concept that an effective passer can pass immediately from the position in which the ball is received. This ability keeps the opposition from assuming a more favorable stance to intercept. Some of the greatest passers today pass to a teammate with a volleyball type pass. The ball just touches the fingers before release. This is a very rapid pass.

The "look-away pass" is employed by most good passers (Figure 4-11). The late Jerome "Shocky" Needy, a guard from the University of Oklahoma in the middle 1930s, gave defensive players all kinds of trouble by first seeing an open teammate as he dribbled down the floor. Without ever looking again directly at the open player, he passed right to him.

Figure 4-11. Look away pass.

Most modern players make use of this pass when two offensive players are going to the basket, often on a fast break, against one defensive player. The look-away pass is effective because the defensive player is forced to shift the body's center of gravity in the direction of the look. A shift in the wrong direction prevents the defensive player from correcting the mistake quickly. The ball may be passed before the correction is made.

The ability to pass on the run is one aspect of an excellent passer's skills. To pass on the dribble just as the ball bounces up from the floor is an added skill that keeps a defensive player from being too aggressive.

Cooper and Siedentop listed 10 principles of passing performance (4, p. 39).

1. Good passers make optimum use of peripheral vision.

2. Except in unusual situations, passes should be executed so the ball is received at waist to chest high elevation. A lob may be used over a defensive player who is fronting a teammate. A tall player may receive the passed ball high and out in front, especially if the defensive player is guarding from the rear. Also, the ball may be passed to the opposite side of the defensive player's position.

3. Except in unusual situations, passes should be delivered in as near a horizontal plane as possible. Gravity prohibits a true horizontal flight path, but a path with too much of an arch is dangerously open for interception.

4. There are several vulnerable areas on a defensive player's body by which passes can be thrown, depending on the defender's stance and hand positions. Usually the passer tries over the shoulder of the down arm, the open area under the raised arm, the above area of the head when the arms are both lowered or extended to the side, and between the legs in a wide feet position.

5. The closer a defensive player is to the passer, the easier it is to pass by him or her. The ball can be moved faster than the defensive player can move the arms and hands, since the offensive player moves through a smaller range and knows where to throw the ball.

6. A passer must be able to pass quickly and forcefully from any position.

7. A definite passing target should be selected. Normally, the pass should be to the side away from the defensive player. If the intended pass recipient is much taller or can jump much higher than the defensive player, then the pass may be thrown to a high target, such as hands extended above the head. The receiving player may often come to meet the ball to get away from a defensive player.

8. Knee extension, slight shoulder mediation, and forearm pronation contribute to the force (velocity) of the ball when it is thrown.

9. Increased wrist and forearm pronation results in greater velocity of the ball at release.

10. The objective in passing is to get the ball to a teammate quickly without telegraphing the intended path to the defensive player.

To this list, the following principles should be added.

11. All two-hand passes are actually one-hand, in that the dominant hand comes off the ball last.

12. The index and middle fingers are in contact with the ball the longest.

There are commonalities in the mechanics of the throwing–pushing action in the four most–used passes. The chest pass, the overhead pass, the baseball pass, and the bounce pass will be analyzed.

Chest Pass

In a chest pass, a player releases the ball at or near chest level. The ball is gripped with the fingers spread on the sides of the ball to the rear. The thumbs are placed to the rear, parallel to each other. The ball is moved backward in order for the hands to be extended before being flexed. Some would call this "cocking the wrist," which is not accurate, since the wrist bones move relatively little. The thumbs come off the ball as it moves forward. The hands apply impetus from behind (Figure 4–12). The thumbs do not contribute to the forward propulsion, but aid in gripping the ball before release.

Figure 4–12. Chest or push pass.

The muscles that control the hand and fingers originate on the forearm and cross the wrist bones. Extending the hands stretches those muscles, causing them to contract over a longer distance. More force is generated.

74

To increase the velocity of the ball at release, a step forward is used. However, the time element is increased, so a quick pass is replaced by one with more velocity. Increased velocity may also be gained if the arms and hands move through a wider range of motion. Again, this takes more time and may allow the defensive player to correctly anticipate the direction of the pass.

Accurate, relatively long passes are characterized by lengthy follow-through, a sign of great force. The backs of the hands end up within six inches or closer to each other because of the pronation of the forearms and hands.

In a bullet-like pass, the velocity is great enough to partially offset the pull of gravity. However, the ball does not travel in a straight line. The angle of release is elevated enough so that the ball arrives at receiver's waist, or just above or below, depending on the defensive player's position. The flight path is curved.

The follow-through after a short pass is likewise short. This indicates a reduced velocity, with a small amount of elbow extension and hand flexion and pronation.

A ball passed with high velocity to a teammate in close proximity is difficult to catch. Attenuation of the ball is nearly impossible. In this case, "a soft pass often turnest away errors." The reverse would be true in a long pass, especially one that goes cross-court. Cross-court passes, however, are risky.

Overhead Pass

The overhead pass is executed similarly to a chest pass. There is knee extension, medial rotation, and forearm and hand pronation. Often it is not possible to step forward during the throw, so velocity at release is generated almost without transfer of momentum from the step. Offensive guards out on the court frequently use this pass, especially if they are tall and can see over the defensive players.

The ball is held initially above the head. As the pass is executed, the elbows flex and the hands extend, moving the ball backward before it is moved forward to release. Strong forearms and hands make for greater release velocity. The positions of the hands and the thumbs are the same as those in the chest pass, but follow-through is not as pronounced. The release velocity is not as great, and the flight path is usually forward and more downward, which takes advantage of gravity.

Bounce Pass

The bounce pass is intended for use in situations where the ball strikes the floor before a defensive player can intercept it. The ball goes under the defensive player's arms and rebounds to a teammate. A look away turn of the head makes the pass more effective.

The beginning of this pass is identical to that of the chest pass if the bounce pass is delivered with two hands. The ball may be released with a back spin for a higher angle of reflection. This uses friction when the ball hits the floor to reduce the ball's speed. If top spin is used, the ball bounces off the floor lower, travels a greater distance, and is harder to catch. Side spin passes are used occasionally by passers. The ball velocity at release must be sufficient to force the ball to travel downward, hit the floor, and bounce to a teammate. Delivery time is increased. More force from the legs, arms, and trunk is needed than in a chest pass. The bounce from the floor is not always accurate. Some coaches limit the use of the bounce pass.

In the one-hand bounce pass, less spin can be administered to the ball. It will rebound from the floor because of the reduced friction.

Baseball Pass

The baseball pass is usually used when the objective is to move the ball quickly over distances greater than half the court. Situations that call for this pass include a fast break following a defensive rebound, an out-of-bounds situation under the basket due to a turnover, or after a successful goal by the offensive team. The ball can be thrown by a strong passer the entire length of the court. A hook shot may be used in these situations, but it has sideward spin and curves in the air. Upon contact with the floor, it moves in the direction of the spin.

In the baseball pass, the ball is held from behind in the right hand (for right-handed players) and low (the extent depends on the distance the ball is to be thrown). The left hand helps to support the ball. As throwing begins, the fingers of the right hand are spread and face upward. The feet are apart, with the left foot slightly in front of the right.

The direction of the front foot helps dictate the direction of the throw. The ball is moved to the rear, then the elbow is flexed. Next the ball is moved farther back behind the right shoulder. If possible, a small step by the left foot may be taken before release. The knees may be flexed. Usually the passer faces his body toward the court. The body action may start with the left side slightly rotated to the rear so that as the action takes place, the hips may turn in the direction of the throw.

The small step, the rotation of the hips, and the wide range of the movement of the arms all add momentum to the ball as it is released. As the arm and hand move forward to begin the release, the elbow extends and moves to the side at shoulder height. The ball is released a slight distance in front of the body.

The baseball pass may be thrown by a player who is in the air, but the distance the ball travels will be reduced. The player would turn to face the court before jumping.

The follow-through indicates that as the release takes place, the thumb and the left hand are not touching the ball. The knees are extended from a flexed position, the right shoulder is rotated medially, and the forearm and hand are pronated. The greater the extent of these actions, the greater the velocity at release. Velocity is highest at release; afterwards, velocity decreases due to gravity and air resistance.

SHOOTING

Shooting in basketball is, as Wooden said, "a pass to the basket." (19, p. 71) Yet it is different from passing in that the target area is stationary and elevated, not moving. The impetus given the ball at release is not the same, since the passed ball is thrown with as much force as the receiver can manage. The ball shot at a basket is released quickly, but softly, with an upward thrust. Brancazio said that a shooter is launching the "projectile up an incline." However, some of the mechanics of passing are present in shooting.

Shooting is one of the most difficult skills in basketball. A player usually has only a few tenths of a second to make decisions on range, angle, and velocity. it takes years of practice for the action to become automatic. The player should not have to think with higher brain mechanisms while shooting. It should be intuitive.

Changes in shooting style are difficult to perfect once players reach high school age or beyond. Under stress, any player may revert to an incorrect motion that became habitual in childhood, even though the motion was corrected.

Some players are shooters and some scorers. Certain shooters are mechanically sound in execution but not reliable scorers for several reasons, including slowness, lack of concentration, and lack of strength. Scorers are players who score in any way possible, regardless of mechanics and shooting position.

Cousy distinguishes between aiming and sighting. This may only be a matter of semantics. He attempts to show that aiming is equally divided between the shooter and the target, as in aiming a gun. Sighting is the act of locating, focusing, and determining the target in space (5, p. 36, 37). All of the necessary calculations are performed before the ball is projected toward the goal. This was supported in a study indicating that players shot very well regardless of whether they could see the basket, as long as they could determine where the basket was by where they were on the court.

Mental imagery is involved in this process. Through training, the player learns to prepare for shooting by reflecting on the image of the action.

The muscles performing the act of shooting have a memory in a sense. The feeling of a successful motion is recorded in the mind and body. When the motion is duplicated to any degree later, the player will recognize the feeling.

Shooting is a type of specialized throwing with certain restrictions and modifications. In modern basketball, the dominant hand is the last to contact the ball as it is released toward the basket. Yet, in shots used in the past, (the underhand shot, two-hand set shot, and two-hand jump shot), the hands and fingers of the dominant hand also were last to give impetus to the ball before it was released. The same is true of the one-hand set, the jump shot, the hook shot, the underhand layup, the scoop shot, and the push one-hand layup. The patterns in past and present styles are remarkably similar.

Cooper and Siedentop listed a number of shooting principles.
1. "Good shooters should always aim at a specific target." The target area might be the front of the rim of the basket, the back of the rim, the open area within the basket, or a spot on the backboard. In the past, the good shooter often used the backboard as a target while 15 to 20 feet from the basket or at an angle from the basket. The wooden backboard had a greater coefficient of friction than glass with a spinning ball, so greater accuracy was possible. Close in shots such as layups and even hook shots can rebound off a glass board into the basket if thrown to the correct spot.
2. "Good shooters should maintain constant eye focus on the target until the ball is released." If a shooter raises his or her eyes to watch the ball (in turn raising the neck, upper chest, and head), the center of gravity is also raised, which changes the flight path of the ball.
3. "The ball should always be 'wiggled' if possible." This activates nerve endings in the fingers and the proprioceptors in the joints to give

the player an acute awareness or feel of the ball and its position in the hands. It should occur even in a closely guarded situation. At the very least, this mental conditioning should help to relax the shooting hand and arm.

4. "The shooter should not hold his or her body in a fixed position for very long before releasing the ball (especially the arms and hands)." Remaining in a state of readiness to perform a gross body action, such as foul shooting, for more than 1.7 seconds causes the body to lose some of its fluid muscular coordination and efficiency.

5. "The ball should be delivered with a reverse spin in most instances." The reverse spin, due to friction, reduces the speed of the ball, which rebounds from the backboard or basket rim more softly and higher than it would without spin. It is easier to rebound defensively and tip in offensively, or it may strike the goal or backboard and still go in the basket.

6. "The better the shooter, the more intense is the concentration on the act of shooting." The good shooter is prepared to shoot at the basket when within range and partially free from a defender. The great shooter-passer can change from a shooter to passer or the reverse within fractions of a second. Such a player is rare, since the body needs to change movement patterns rapidly and intuitively. If the player has to think before acting, the opportunity to shoot or pass may be lost.

7. "Shooting is characterized by slight but almost unnoticed medial shoulder rotation, elbow extension, forearm pronation, and wrist flexion." These actions are barely detectable in shooting, except when players shoot at long range, but they are part of the joints' motion. They can be seen as the ball is released, when the forefinger points to the basket and moves below the other fingers.

Shooting is a combination of throwing and pushing. The action in modern basketball rarely takes place farther than 20 feet from the basket. Therefore, the less pronounced the limbs' actions, the more accurate the toss and the slower the ball velocity in flight. The knees are flexed, but not to the degree of a shot putter's. The shoulder, elbow, forearm, and hand actions are also less pronounced. The release is slightly out in front, so particular movements are not as visible as they are in baseball.

8. "The longer the distance from the basket the ball is delivered, the more pronounced is the forearm pronation." More force is needed on release for the ball to go the distance. Unfortunately, the shooter may

use a lower angle of release because there is not enough force for the ball to reach the basket if shot at a higher angle. A 43-degree angle is best for distance shooting. The player should drop the ball lower, flex the knees more, and move the body in a forceful half-turn. More joints become involved. All this makes a long shot more difficult, but the higher angle and softer shot are significant advantages.

9. "Technically, the higher the arch, the more chance the ball has to go into the basket." This involves a compromise. An angle higher than 70 degrees means more force is being exerted by the shooter. Softness (lowvelocity and backspin) may be sacrificed to gain a high entry. A very low angle or release (30 degrees or less), however, may cause the shooter to exert too much force with not enough spin.

Brancazio has stated that since the shooter launches his shot up an incline, the angle of the release is between 45 and 52 degrees. Hay (8, p.218) and Hudson (11) think the maximum angle should be between 58 and 62 degrees. Brancazio (3, p.309) thinks that the long range shot calls for a lower angle of release than a short shot. Taller players usually release closer to 45 degrees from the floor than do shorter players, he maintains.

10. "As a player moves up in competitive levels, he or she must be able to deliver shots with greater quickness to have greater opportunity to achieve success in shooting." This is especially true for smaller players. To "press" when shooting activates unnecessary muscles and destroys consistency and accuracy.

The cutting angles of the offensive player must be sharp to keep the defensive player from running shorter distances on defense. The good shooter learns to cut more directly toward the basket before receiving the ball from a teammate in preparation for a shot.

The most popular and the most written about shot is the one-hand jump shot. It began as a so-called two-hand jump, but it was actually one-hand since the dominant hand was the last to touch the ball upon release.

Gates and Holt found the following information concerning jump shooters.

1. More successful shooters demonstrated a greater angle at the shoulders on release, from a lateral view.

2. More successful shooters used a smaller elbow angle at the start of the shot than the poorer shooters.

3. A greater back spin during flight was associated with high performance shooters.

80

4. The successful shooters demonstrated a closer alignment of the upper arm with the vertical at release.

Cousy states that the jump shot can be executed from "a standing position, off a dribble, and after a cut is made and the ball received." (5, P. 46) While the mechanics of delivery are the same in each instance, the mechanics prior to the launching of the shot are different.

Many experts believe that a one-step method is the best to use in a jump shot approach from a dribble or when the player has just received a pass. The front foot is planted, then the trail foot joins it. The player jumps by flexing the knees and pushing against the floor with the feet. The body faces the basket in shooting the jump shot. Students of shooting call this position "squaring up" to the basket with feet nearly parallel in the air.

This "squared up" position, or right shoulder rotation, which may be a better description, is assumed by all good performers in throwing and striking an object. Gates and Holt found that the best shooters were slightly less "squared" to the basket than the poorer players. The head turns slightly in the direction of the dominant eye focusing on the basket.

Depending on what the shooter desires, the knees may be flexed or extended while in the air. A quick, low jump may be necessary to fool an offensive player. Before takeoff, the feet should be 6 to 10 inches apart and under the center of gravity.

Players are said to drift in the air as they shoot. An off center jump begins while the player is still on the floor. A tilt of the head, shoulder movement, or a change in the center of gravity will change the direction of the flight of the ball. While in the air the player may move body parts, but the path of the center of gravity is not changed.

The amount of time a player can remain in the air is known as hang time. A good hang time is about .30 of a second. The player will manipulate the body (particularly the arms and the legs) to move the center of gravity up. The player must keep the head, shoulders, and trunk over the feet. A longer hang time may help a player elude an opponent.

Experts believe that the starting position of the elbow and hand are the keys to good shooting. The release position of the elbow is more important than the starting position. The elbow of the shooting arm should be pointed toward the basket on release. Lehmann says that the elbow should be kept within the plane of the body and should not move laterally.

When a player grips the ball for a shot, the ball should rest on the fingers. However, many modern players have hands so large that the ball rests partly on the palm. Some authorities maintain that a grip involving the palm allows for better control. Sharman believes the thumb and the index finger of the shooting hand should form a V and should be in line with the shoulder of the shooting arm (Figure 4-13). Which target to shoot the ball toward has been a subject of much debate. Choices favored by various experts include the back of the rim, the front of the rim, just over the front of the rim, and just short of the rim. Good shooters are consistent in the initial selection of the target area. However, if they miss several times, they adjust by raising or lowering the angle of release and by shooting slightly beyond or short of the target.

Figure 4-13. V position of ball in shooting (by permission from Sharman, Bill. Englewood Cliffs, NJ: Prentice-Hall Inc.,1965, p 34).

A player's location on the floor helps to determine the target. From the corner of the court the shooter will aim exclusively at the basket; in front of the basket, the shooter will also aim toward the backboard.

At what point is the ball released in the jump shot? The strength of the shooter, the distance from the basket, and the position and size of the defenders are among variables that determine release points.

Most experts, including Brancazio, Hess, Martin, and Macauley, favor release at the peak of the jump. At this juncture, the upward momentum and the weight force due to gravity are zero. (Although the pull of gravity is not actually zero, its effect is neutralized at this point.) It is easier to shoot under these circumstances.

A player who is 35 feet or more from the basket may release the ball on the way up in jumping. Gorton found that college women released the ball going up, and men released at the peak. Perhaps the new smaller ball and better skills have changed this situation for women players.

The follow–through in shooting is a continuation of the shooting procedure. It prevents the shooter from stopping too soon and causing a jerky motion. It makes shooting a rhythmic, natural, and smooth transference of action from one component part to another.

A variety of other shots, including the one–hand set shot, the hook, the front layup, the scoop, the reverse layup, the free throw, and even the dunk and fade–away shots employ some of the same mechanical elements as the jump shot. Players consider target area selection, pronation of the forearm and hand, maintenance of head and shoulder level, eye focus on the target, and follow–through.

Future in–the–air shots will probably be executed with the player holding the ball above and behind the head in a jump shot while facing the basket. The hook shot will be combined with a jump shot by inside players. These actions will be taken to prevent defenders from blocking shots. More shots will be taken while the player is moving. The player will need to control the speed of movement at release and the angle of projection.

Foul Shooting

Foul shooting is similar to one-hand jump shooting in that this 15-foot shot involves a balanced stance, usually with the feet parallel and shoulder width apart. The head remains stationary. There is shoulder medial rotation and pronation of the forearm and hand. The elbow faces the basket at release, and the body of the shooter is "squared up" to the basket.

Hudson found that characteristics of women players included a high point of release, a well-balanced weight distribution, and minimal trunk inclination. The better players had higher angles of projection (62 degrees) and quicker releases without high velocity.

Cooper and Siedentop presented several principles of performance in foul shooting.

1. "The player should dry off the fingertips. The ball is loosely held to establish a sense of feel. The ball is shaken with the hands by moving the wrist, or it is bounced on the floor once or twice. Such movements release tension...." The player observes teammates to see that all are off the foul lines.

2. "The feet are placed in a stride position close to the foul line, with the right foot in front of the left (for right-handed shooters). The toes

of the right foot should be pointing inward, and the toes of the left slightly out. The head is kept down to watch correct foot placement, and the ball is kept just over the head or close to the waist to avoid creating tension in the arms.... The ball rests on the fingers rather than the palm of the hands."

3. "The player takes a deep breath." This is relaxing and also prevents the chest area from moving during the shot.

4. "The player looks at the goal and focuses on a targetpoint. The head is up and the back straight."

5. With the knees slightly bent, the ball is brought back and down. The wrists are flexed, then the ball is released out in front of the body. If more than 1.7 seconds elapse in this ready position, the player may become tense and the accuracy of the shot may be affected. The follow–through is rhythmic as the knees bend then extend. The arms are pointed directly at the basket in the follow–through.

6. The ball should be released with a slight backspin, which will make it easier to catch on the rebound and may cause the ball to go into the basket off the board or back rim. Estimates are that a correctly delivered shot makes several revolutions before it reaches the goal.

7. The ball must be tossed softly in harmony with the rhythm of the entire body.

8. "The eyes should not follow the ball in flight, but should fix on a target."

9. The shooter should avoid stepping toward the basket too soon by keeping the toes of both feet on the floor until the shot has been made. The heel is lifted off the floor during the action.

10. The shooter should keep extraneous movements to a minimum to aid in the accuracy of the shot. A rhythmic, smooth movement ensures a soft, accurate shot.

CHAPTER 5

Game Time: Player Movement Skills in Action

To prepare this chapter, I viewed game films, took notes at games, watched games on television, and discussed ideas with coaches and other students of basketball. Some of the statements herein may have some bearing on strategy and coaching procedures. I attempt to discuss primarily certain individual player skills under selected categories, but I do not avoid implications of these actions for teams. In fact, it is often difficult in a game situation to separate the team and an individual player.

Some topics that are mentioned in Chapter 4 are omitted here. In some instances there has been a combining of topics and ideas. However, some new ideas are presented since action in games presents many unusual versions of basic fundamental movements due to the defense. Also, most movements are not isolated, but involve several skills in one action such as dribbling, jumping, and shooting. The reader should refer to the information in Chapter 3 and 4 for understanding and clarity. The physical principles governing action in games are the same, with some modification, as those mentioned in these previous chapters. Explanation as to why certain actions are made is my desire in presenting the information.

Since this chapter involves game situations, it was thought best to include only selected happenings. It is restricted to a brief and concise discussion of most of the fundamental moves.

GUARDING

Some teams with quick, aggressive players who have sound defensive skills use defensive techniques such as the press to key their offensive efforts. Effective use of the press, traps, and tight defensive positions is essential to these teams' success.

Press in this sense means that, individually or collectively, defensive player(s) get as close as possible to an offensive player (with or without the ball) and attempt to deflect the passed ball or prevent the ball from being passed to a given player. Sometimes this involves two or more defensive players guarding one offensive player (double and triple teaming). A trap occurs when two or more players surround one offensive player often along the sideline or baseline. Frequently, these situations occur in the back court. When an offensive player is trapped along the sideline or baseline by a defensive player, the effect is the same as if two, not one, defensive players were trapping. it reduces maneuvering, including passing possibilities. Smart offensive players try to avoid being forced into these situations. Georgetown and University of Iowa employ this kind of press very successfully.

These maneuvers reduce the number of passing lanes available to the offensive passer as well as obscure the teammates to whom a pass could be made. Furthermore, the close guarding position often prevents the passer from using deception in the pass as well as reduces the range of motion of the throw (pass), thus, causing the velocity of the ball to be low. If an offensive player panics, the pass is thrown too quickly or is often inaccurate or thrown out-of-bounds or into the hands of a defensive player. If no error is committed, at least great energy is expended to avoid the press. Late in the game, the mechanics of jumping, shooting, and guarding may be affected by fatigue.

To offset the effectiveness of the press, rapid passing of the ball even from the back court to the front court, negates some of its advantages. A small, quick dribbler, especially against defensive players who lack quickness, may "break" the press because of his or her velocity and low center of gravity, which make stops and starts easier.

Two present day college players are small with their centers of gravity below the trapping players. They frequently squeeze between the trappers and escape, often receiving a foul shot in addition. Reversing direction before the trap is set and avoiding the sideline and endlines helps in eluding traps.

On the other hand, quick, relentless, defensive pressing players will annihilate slow, poor dribblers and poor ball handlers as well as those not prepared for such tactics. Several teams in recent years have surprised their opponents by the use of traps and presses.

Thus, it is usually difficult to contain, press, or trap a good ball handler, either in the front or back court, especially if the player is quick. This type of player can change direction quickly, throwing the defensive player off and causing the defensive player to move in the wrong direction. Several universities and professional teams have guards who are such quick and elusive dribblers that the press is not often successful. If the guards are not quick and good dribblers, they must be good passers or their teams are in for long, frustrating games.

To avoid leaving the floor and jumping into the air in response to a fake by an offensive player, the defensive player firmly plants the feet and watches out of the corner of the eye for the offensive player to bend at the knees, which comes before a jump. A player in the air is helpless to do any movement of consequence while airborne. Arms and legs can be moved but are usually not very effective in, for example, deterring a shot at the basket. Until the airborne player returns to the floor, there can be no real movement fore or aft by the feet. The offensive player may dribble, pass, and even shoot if he or she waits until the defensive player is descending or at least until the defender's feet leave the floor (Figure 5-1).

Figure 5-1. Shooting against an airborne guard.

The defensive player may move up very close to the offensive player to prevent a fake or to lower the center of gravity to be in position to prevent a drive to the basket. A player taller than the shooter may be patient enough to block the shot by jumping into the air just after the shooter starts the shot. This is a matter of timing.

A top offensive guard in the Big Ten Conference is an excellent faker. Frequently, this action frees him for shots or passes not otherwise available because defensive players jump into the air too soon. Good defense is played by moving the feet concurrently, not by leaping in the air at every pretense.

Turnovers are often caused by mechanical error and poor judgment on the part of offensive players. Strong guards are alert to capitalize on these mistakes.

A good defensive player may quickly step into the passing lane and steal the ball. The guard may appear to be too relaxed but at the last moment puts the body into action with intensity, as would a sprinter in a standup start position. Often it is a matter of determining the passing lanes, and the height, speed, and direction of the pass, and being mentally alert to any cues the passer may give to indicate the proposed flight of the ball.

The defensive player notes if the offensive player holds the ball carelessly or is not very alert and if the intended recipient is not prepared. The receiving player protects the path of the flight by moving the body between the defensive player and oncoming ball. A slow, off-target pass is the easiest to intercept. This happens at least three or four times at each game. The defensive player's position should be to the inside of the potential receiver.

A star guard for the University of Michigan basketball team is quick and very alert. If the opposing team's passer throws a low velocity or off-target pass, he will pick it off because of his anticipation, inside position, or both. In recent games, a defensive player was able to strike the ball out of an offensive player's hands and the ball traveled in the air parallel to the floor a good distance. This meant that the ball was hit with the closed fist or hand at the ball's center. The arm striking the ball was in an underhand (supine) position rather than overhand (pronated) which prevented a foul assessment.

A recent check by a group of graduate students and me revealed that 8 out of 10 fouls called in a 1987 game were, in our collective opinion, caused by the defensive player being out of position (a half step behind a player or had overshifted too far). Many of the fouls were called because the defensive player reached with the arms instead of first moving the feet to get in front of the offensive player before attempting to knock the ball from the hands or reaching out with hands or arms to prevent the player from making a cut.

Waving the hand in front of a taller post player is usually done with the off-hand with the defensive player being tight from a side position. This defensive player will have to switch from one side to the other as the ball is moved from one side of the court to the other. This action is a common sight at many games (Figure 5-2).

Figure 5-2. Waving in front of a taller post player.

Fronting the offensive player does work if there is weak side help from teammates. This technique is seen often in most colleges and professional games.

Playing the post player from a rear position can be successful if the defensive player can out-jump the offensive player. Strict attention to cues signaling movement is necessary. If the offensive player is not a good shooter, then screening out and having the defender's center of gravity placed below that of the offensive player will make rebounding easier. At two recent college games (male and female teams), the post player was permitted to shoot and did not score in repeated attempts. The defensive post player simply blocked the shooter out and got the rebound.

In a recent game, one player was played tight (close) and another was played loose (soft). The latter player scored 31 points because he was open with no one very close to him. In a recent televised game, a very fast guard was guarded too closely and was able to drive around the opponent and scored almost at will. The opposing player was slower than the offensive player and couldn't react quickly enough to stop the drive. He was faked out of position. His center of gravity shifted in one direction, the offensive player went the opposite way.

JUMPING

In basketball, jumpers are classified as poor, quick, and high jumpers. Many times a poor jumper who is in a good position is as effective as a high leaper. Two eastern colleges met, and the team with the poorest jumpers out rebounded the team with the great leapers because they screened the leapers off and prevented them from going to the boards. The high leapers look spectacular and, if not defended properly, will get many rebounds. They should especially be effective on the defensive boards. However, ordinary jumpers such as Larry Bird of the Boston Celtics are able to know where the ball is and get inside the leapers.

A quick leaper leaves the floor in a shorter span of time than a higher jumper but the impulse is not as great, so the quick jumper is not as high off the floor. However, most rebounds are fielded below the rim. Thus, the quick jumper has the advantage over slow, low–jumping opponents. One university won the NCAA title in recent years with a sixth player who was a quick leaper. Incidentally, he was selected to the all tournament team.

PASSING

Passing rapidly by offensive players is an asset because defensive players cannot react and move as fast as a passed ball. This was evident when two eastern college teams were playing recently. One team had a lead with 4 minutes to go in the game. The team in the lead passed the ball for approximately 32 seconds (45 seconds allotted for each possession) without the defensive members being able to steal the ball during the first 2 minutes. Then they fouled in the last 2 minutes, but never could move fast enough to intercept a pass. Both good college and professional teams are able to pass the ball in a double teaming situation so rapidly the players double teaming cannot move fast enough to move back and cover their original assigned players or territories. This occurred on 6 different occasions in a recent college game with the offensive teams scoring 3 times out of 6.

If an offensive player "telegraphs" where a ball is being thrown, the defensive player takes a reading on the height, speed, and direction and often has no trouble intercepting. In a recent college game a point guard looked where the ball was to be passed four times in a row. Consequently, it went to an opponent in all four occasions. A "look away" pass should have been used.

In a recent high school game, offensive players tried in several instances to bounce the ball into and through a compact group of defensive players and were unsuccessful. Normally, this attack method is not advocated unless the passers use great deception and throw the ball with good velocity. The defensive players have such a short distance to travel and the throw takes longer time to be completed.

The bounce pass is effective when a teammate is partially open. The defensive players have to shift their eyes downward to locate the ball and then move their feet. (See Chapter 4 on the number of bounced passes used in a game.)

If a player jumps into the air with the ball and attempts to pass, he or she may not find an open recipient. Gravity pulls the player down to the floor, and the ball may have to be passed wildly to avoid a traveling call. It is often unwise to jump and then attempt to pass. Four times during a viewed game the "ball was lost" by the offensive team because one of the players was in the air and could not find any teammate to receive the pass.

In almost every game, there occurs a situation whereby a player attempts to keep the ball from being declared out-of-bounds. Usually, the ball bounces in the air beyond the side or endlines. To retrieve the ball a player jumps in the air from the court area and attempts to throw the ball into the court before landing on the floor out-of-bounds. It is estimated that more than 60 percent of the time the ball is caught by a member of the opposing team if the retrieved ball is thrown blindly. Recently, in a professional game, a star player retrieved the ball in the air out-of-bounds and was able to turn in the air (the turning action began before leaving the floor), face the court, locate a teammate, and throw the ball to him. This is so much better than throwing the ball without having a target in mind.

A long throw to an open player on a fast break normally is thrown toward the center of the court, rather than the sidelines. The receiver is thus closer to the basket in the center.

On a fast break, the offensive team uses three running lanes up the court and tries to keep the ball near the center. As the players approach the basket, this permits a pass to be made to either a teammate or a shot to be taken at the basket. The dribbler passes or stops to shoot, depending on the movement of the defense. Good teams make use of this maneuver five or more times in a game.

The effective use of the lob pass over a zone defense is evident even when passing to an offensive player for an "alleyoop," Passing rapidly in the front court and side portions of the offensive court causes the players in the zone to move and expose the weaknesses which are usually in the middle and along the endline. Also, there are frequently open spaces between the zone players. In a recent game the offensive team players were so clever in passing rapidly and disguising their intent against the zone that they outscored their opponents by 20 points in the second half.

Passes against a zone go over, under, around, but not through the players. The zone players defend a territory, but they can only shift their bodies a certain distance in a given time. A penetrating guard is often hampered by a zone when two players block the entry. This happened in a college game because the passing abilities of the other four players were not good enough to take advantage of the over-shifting.

Good passing is the best method to use in beating a zone, but against a zone and even a man-to-man defense, a good dribbler must penetrate the first line of defense. This opens up passing lanes if the second line of defense converges. This occurs many times in a game if the first penetration is accomplished.

Several colleges (both men and women teams) have been placing a tall defensive player in front of the passer, passing in from out-of-bounds along the endline, especially if the offensive team has very little time left in the game and needs to go the length of the court to score. Since the height of the defensive player affects the passer and may cause the execution of the pass to be less effective, the passer may move along the endline or pass to teammates who are out-of-bounds. This can only be done if the out-of-bounds is a result of an opponent's successful goal from the field or foul line. In out-of-bound situations due to other circumstances (such as deflected passes) the passer must remain stationary as the inbound pass is made. A long pass in such a situation is sometimes successful. If a pass is made to a nearby teammate from out-of-bounds, the passer may receive the ball back immediately after returning to the court. Screens are used to set free a player to receive a pass. The quick delivery of a pass to a fast player usually eases movement toward the front court from the endline position. If a team doesn't possess a tall defensive player, often the coach has two players guarding one player or a zone defense is set up to try to prevent a successful in-bound pass.

An offensive player who sees the entire court and finds an open receiver possesses good peripheral vision. One midwestern university has a player on its team who is only 5'7", but his court vision is astounding. When this player enters the game, things begin to happen. The teammates receive unexpected passes from him, and the defensive players are befuddled. Such a player resembles a bridge player who knows where all the cards are. This basketball player knows where the teammates are at all times, doesn't look directly at them, and passes unselfishly to the open player for the benefit of the team.

SHOOTING

A study of game film sent to the author, as well as close scrutiny of several games, revealed a number of facts about shooting.

Shots should not be attempted when a player's body isn't under control and ready. Off-balance shots are ineffective because all or a part of the body is moving in a direction that is not in line with the basket. Two out of 20 off-balanced shots in the film were successful and these were just luck.

The arms extend then flex or flex then extend in both shooting and passing. Layups in a game situation provide particularly clear examples of this concept (Figure 5-3).

Figure 5-3. Lay up.

Offensive players sometimes hang in the air before shooting to confuse defensive players. Pumps or double pumps make guarding more difficult. Eight times during a game between two top college teams, pump or double pumps were utilized.

Small players frequently dribble toward taller players, stop, then shoot directly over their opponents to score. The film I viewed pinpointed a small player five times during one of the games in which he drove at the taller player and was either fouled or scored. Taller and often larger players prefer to be a short distance away from smaller players, either to one side or the other or even behind, instead of up close and in front. Dribbling right at a larger opponent does not allow the big player to guard two players at once. If the bigger player commits to the driver, the ball may be passed to a teammate.

Tension affects the mechanics of play, especially shooting. The nervous system tells the muscles to shoot. If a player is tense, however, conflicting messages are also reaching the muscles. This will usually bring about poor mechanics. Players who are relaxed and confident usually play with sounder mechanical skills than players who are tentative and nervous. Smart defensive players capitalize on the mistakes of tense opponents.

Under normal circumstances, good shooters play the percentages and shoot at manageable ranges. When a defensive effort causes a player to move out and shoot beyond a customary distance, mechanics are sometimes impaired. The shooting arm, legs, and head are not properly aligned. This is known as pressing or forcing in an attempt to score. It is rarely successful as was evident in a high school game I viewed when a player tried to score from beyond her range. She made just 2 of 11 shots.

High percentage shots are normally taken close to the basket. However, the distance from the basket varies according to a player's shooting ability. Most good players make close-in shots 70 percent of the time, and 40 to 50 percent of the shots are made from 15 to 18 feet.

Sometimes a player misses a shot on a layup because he or she expects contact from a defensive player. The anticipation distracts the offensive player and destroys the rhythm of the shooting action. The player shoots too soon or too late. Also, concentration on shooting is lost or at least affected adversely. A good but young player in a Big Ten game heard "footsteps" and missed a possible game-winning shot because of this situation. The more experienced and mature a player is, the less likely the player is to let this happen. Smart shooters concentrate on shooting, regardless of defensive actions. Players practice shooting under game conditions, with and without defensive contact, to prepare for such eventualities.

When a player moves the head and shoulders up in a pump fake, there is a tendency to move the feet. The center of gravity is slightly elevated and the player may feel unbalanced. Experienced players concentrate on keeping the feet firmly planted during a faking motion. The best shooter on a Big Ten Conference college team uses this procedure.

Offensive high school stars may find it difficult to score in college basketball. The defense closes off shooting angles and driving lanes. Players adjust to the new conditions by cutting to the basket in tighter curves and by shooting faster. Two great high school players joined a Big Ten team. One adjusted to the tougher playing environment and is a great college scorer; the other one is playing but not able to score at the high school scoring pace because of lack of adjustment.

There are many openings for shots or passes after a foiled offensive play, movement disturbance, or fumble. Alert players take advantage of such possibilities. Good shooters shoot as soon as opportunities occur, before the defense is set. Sometimes it is necessary for a player to shoot off the wrong foot to deceive and to release the ball over a taller player. Two good players in the Pacific Coast Conference have mastered this technique.

In playing against a zone, good strategy and mechanics call for the offensive team's best outside shooter (especially if the shooter is small) to shoot from the opposite side of the court away from the other team's best shot blocker. This is true especially when the defense uses a zone. A college coach friend of mine plans his offensive strategy on this premise.

Some shooters jump quickly against good blockers to deceive them. Former Boston Celtic guard Bill Sharman followed this procedure against Wilt Chamberlain (Philadelphia 76er's, 1950's). Until he used this technique, he had many shots blocked by Chamberlain.

Anticipation enables a player to take advantage of an opponent's lack of preparation. For example, an offensive player who expects to shoot after receiving a pass may notice that the posture of the defender is ineffective against a quick shot. An easy score can follow such observation.

Shooting on the run and using a half hook with a jump shot are the new moves in offensive basketball. Several top players are now using them. Defensive players are not now prepared to adequately defend against them. In the future, versatility in shot selection, such as that demonstrated by Larry Bird of the Boston Celtics, Magic Johnson of the Los

Angeles Lakers, and Michael Jordan of the Chicago Bulls, will be in vogue and new defense moves will be developed. The 3-point area in college basketball, the shot clock, and the proposed wide 3-second lane are opening or will open new vistas.

OTHER FACTORS

Falling: Knowing how to fall is important. As a player starts to fall, he or she should relax, cushion the fall with the arms or large part of the body, contact the floor gradually, and fall as if sinking into water. Of course, all this takes place in fractions of a second, but serious injury can be prevented. Two players on one college team and four professional players were severely hurt in one weekend because they fell improperly. On the other hand, there were 12 falls recorded in one game where landing was done properly and no injuries occurred, only bruises.

Fatigue: Tired players exhibit certain characteristics. They bend over and put their hands on their knees during opponents' foul shots, take shorter strides than normal when running, lower their centers of gravity, lean forward, extend the arms laterally (decreasing lift), reduce step frequency, and spread the legs to have a wider base of support. Older players show these symptoms earlier in games than younger athletes. Fatigue is more evident on defense than it is on offense. In a college game this year, a defensive player was assigned to guard a great offensive player exclusively. He was able to keep the offensive player at 2 field goals in 30 minutes, then fatigue set in. The offensive player scored 12 more points in the remaining 10 minutes. In two televised Eastern College Conference games, the pace of the games was so fierce that near the end of the game several of the players were unable to execute the shots and move mechanically correct. The best conditioned team won in both instances.

Speed: When experts debate the advantages of strength versus speed in basketball, speed usually comes out on top, especially in an outside player. Quickness is often more important in basketball than pure speed.

It is difficult to teach quickness, but there are certain mechanical moves a player may do to increase the speed of the first three or four steps. The player should move with a rather long and low first step and make the second and third steps as rapidly as possible without raising the center of gravity very much. The head, shoulders, and hips remain at the same starting height. All great cutting forwards use these techniques to gain advantage over their defensive opponent.

Improvement of hand speed is possible with constant practice. Players with fast hands usually keep their feet apart for a wider base of support. This stance also helps to eliminate movement interference from other body parts, as only the hands should move in the initial action. One outstanding guard in an Eastern College Conference team has been acclaimed as having the quickest hands in the United States.

The use of a shot clock tends to speed up the tempo of play as evidenced in the higher number of total points scored in the average game; but if an offensive team uses too much of the allocated time, panic shots and poor mechanics may result. In viewing games, it was found that the period just before the end of the half, the last 2 or 3 seconds of a 45- or 30-second clock and very near the end of a game, players are successful scoring in only about 5 percent of the time. The body is often out of alignment, the player's feet are not under the center of gravity, and the right shoulder rotation (right hand shooter) doesn't take place.

It is very difficult for players to concentrate on changing movements, such as passing and shooting mechanics, during a game. Psychologists maintain that individuals cannot concentrate on more than one or two things under performance pressure. Players may be able to change minor movements, but too many suggestions from teammates or coaches at the wrong moment may result in poor overall execution. In almost every game, some player is guilty of this mistake.

Finally, some players relax when an opposing team's star fouls out or is ill and can't play. As a result, the defensive and offensive moves may not be mechanically sound. Intensity may drop and defeat may occur. A quote from a college coach in regard to just such a situation: "We lost our hungriness. We lost some of our emotion. We thought we could win easily with the loss of their great player. We quit making things happen. We were complacent and lost when we shouldn't have."

Playing and winning is more than shooting, dribbling, and passing. It involves the will, the desire, the effort, and the intensity.

REFERENCES

Chapter 1

1. Colclaser, Roy A. and Sherra Diehl-Nagle. Materials and Devices for Electrical Engineers and Physicists. McGrawHill, New York, 1984.

2. Cooper, John M., Marlene Adrian, and Ruth Glassow. Kinesiology. The C.V. Mosby Co., St. Louis, 1982.

3. Cooper, John M. and Daryl Siedentop. The Theory and Science of Basketball. Lea and Febiger, Philadelphia, 1969.

4. Devore, Steven and Gregory R. Devore. Sybervision, Muscle Memory Programming. Chicago Review Press, Chicago, IL., 1981.

5. Hay James G. The Biomechanics of Sports Techniques, 2nd Ed. Prentice-Hall, Inc., Englewood Cliffs, N.J., 1978.

6. Kreighbaum, Ellen and Katherine M. Barthels. Biomechanics, A Qualitative Approach for Studying Human Movement, 2nd Ed. Macmillan Publishing Company, New York, 1985.

7. Stull, Robert B. "Study of Hand and Eye Dominance and Coordination of Basketball Players. "Journal of the American Optometric Association, pp. 293-297, 1960.

8. Terauds, Juris and Jerry N. Barham, editors. Biomechanics in Sport, II, (Proceeding of ISBS), Science in Sports Series, Research Center for Sports, Academic Publishers, Del Mar, CA., 1985.

9. Terauds, Juris et. al., editors. Sports Biomechanics, (Proceedings of ISBS), Science in Sports Series, Research Center for Sports, Academic Publishers, Del Mar, CA., 1984.

10. Weiss, Paul. Sport - A Philosophic Inquiry. Southern Illinois University Press, Carbondale and Edwardsville, Feffer and Simons, 1969.

11. Wooden, John R. Practical Modern Basketball, 2nd Ed. John Wiley & Sons, New York, 1980.

Chapter 2

1. Menke, Frank. The Encyclopedia of Sports. A.S. Barnes and Company, New York, 1953.

2. Naismith, James. Basketball It's Origin and Development. Association Press, New York, 1941.

3. Selected Spalding's Official Basketball Guide. American Sports Publishing Company, New York, 1902-1937.

4. Sempert, Dean A." A Study of the Major Rules' Changes in Men's Basketball from 1902-03 to 1953-54". Unpublished Master's Thesis, University of Southern California, Los Angeles, January, 1954.

5. Thanassoulas, George P. Dr. James Naismith, 1861-1939, "Inventor of Basketball." Unpublished Master of Arts Thesis, Wake Forest University, Winston Salem, N.C., 1972.

6. Personal letters from several friends, including Tyke Yates, Alumni Office, Westminister College, Fulton, Missouri, 1985.

Chapter 3

1. Brancazio, Peter J. Sport Science Physical Laws and Optimum Performance. Simon and Schuster, New York, 1983.

2. Dorland, William. Dorland's Illustrated Medical Dictionary. W.B. Saunders, Philadelphia, 1965.

3. Dyson, Geoffry H.G. The Mechanics of Athletics. University of London Press Lts., London, 1977.

4. Gartmann, Heinz. Man Unlimited. Pantheon Books, Inc., New York, 1957.

5. Hay, James. The Biomechanics of Sports Techniques, 2nd. Ed., Prentice-Hall, Inc., Englewood Cliffs, N.J., 1978.

6. Hudson, Jackie. "Shooting Techniques for Small Players," Paper submitted to Athletic Journal, July, 1985. (copy sent author by Dr. Hudson, Rice University).

7. Tricker, R.A. and B.J.K. Tricker. The Science of Movement. American Elsevier Publishing Co., Inc., New York, 1967.

Chapter 4

1. Allsen, P.E. and William Ruffner. "Relationship between the Pass and the Loss of the Ball in Basketball." Athletic Journal 50(1):94, 1969.

2. Bishop, Robert D. and James G. Hay. "Basketball: The Mechanics of Hanging in the Air." Medicine and Science in Sports, Vol. 11, No. 3, 1979.

3. Brancazio, Peter J. Sport Science Physical Laws and Optimum Performance. Simon and Schuster, New York, 1983.

4. Cooper, John M. and Daryl Siedentop. The Theory and Science of Basketball. Lea and Febiger, Philadelphia, 1969.

5. Cousy, Bob and Frank G. Power, Jr. Basketball Concepts and Techniques. Allyn and Bacon, Inc., Boston, 1970.

6. Gates, Gary and L.E. Holt. "The Development of Multiple Linear Regression Equations to Predict Accurancy in Basketball Jump Shooting at Ten and Twenty Feet." Dalhousie University, Halifax, N.S., Canada.

7. Gorton, Beatrice, "Selected Kinetics and Kinematic Factors," Unpublished Doctoral Dissertation. Indiana University, Bloomington, Indiana. Involved in the basketball jump shot, 1978.

8. Hay, James G. The Biomechanics of Sports Techniques, 2nd Ed. Prentice Hall, Inc., Englewood Cliffs, N.J., 1978.

9. Hess, Charles. "Analysis of the Jump Shot." Athletic Journal, November, 1980, 61:3, 30-58.

10. Hoover, Jay A. "A Concentrated Program for Ball Handling Improvement." Coach and Athlete, December, 1975.

11. Hudson, Jackie. "Shooting Techniques for Small Players." Paper submitted to Athletic Journal, July, 1985.

12. Lehmann, George. "Basketball is My Game.", Lessons by Lehmann, Riverside, N.J., 1981.

13. Macauley, Ed. "Anatomy of the Jump Shot." Scholastic Coach, December, 1970, 8-11.

14. Martin, Thomas, P. "Movement Analysis Applied to the Basketball Jump Shot." The Physical Educator, October, 1981, 3:38, 127-133.

15. Newton, C.M. "Ball Handling." Basketball Bulletin, Spring, 1976, 27-28.

16. Seals, "Fundamentals of Ball Handling, Dribbling and Passing." December, 1978, Basketball Clinic.

17. Sempert, Dean. Personal Communication. (Head Basketball Coach, Lewis and Clark College), Portland, Oregon, 1985.

18. Williams, Williams (Chuck). "The Relationship of Selected 'Natural' Traits to Statistical Game Performance in Basketball." Unpublished Dissertation, Indiana University, 1983.

19. Wooden, John R. Practical Modern Basketball, 2nd Ed. John Wiley & Sons, New York, 1980.

Chapter 5

1. Abdul-Jabbar, Kareem and Peter Knobler. Giant Steps, Bantam Books, New York, 1985.

2. Cooper, John M. "Research Implications for Coach and Performer", Biomechanics of Sports II. Edited by Juris Terouds and Jerry N. Barham. Academic Publishers, Del Mar, CA., pp. 80-86.

3. Hay, James G. The Biomechanics of Sports Techniques, 2nd Ed. Prentice-Hall, Inc., Englewood Cliffs, N.J., 1978.

4. Smith, Dean and Robert D. Spears. Basketball Multiple Offense and Defense. Prentice-Hall, Inc., Englewood Cliffs, N.J., 1981.

5. Wooden, John R. Practical Modern Basketball, 2nd Ed. John Wiley & Sons, New York, 1980.